Manage

Accounting

MANAGEMENT ACCOUNTING

A Review of Contemporary Developments

Second Edition

Robert W. Scapens

MACMILLAN

First edition 1985
Reprinted 1987, 1989 (twice), 1990
Second edition 1991

Published by
MACMILLAN EDUCATION LTD
Houndmills, Basingstoke, Hampshire RG21 2XS
and London
Companies and representatives
throughout the world

Printed in Hong Kong

British Library Cataloguing in Publication Data
Scapens, Robert (Robert William) *1946–*
Management accounting: a review of contemporary
developments. — 2nd ed.
1. Management accounting
I. Title
658.1511
ISBN 0–333–55352–7 (hardcover)
ISBN 0–333–55353–5 (paperback)

In memory of W. R. Scapens

Contents

Preface to the First Edition

In 1982 I wrote a survey paper on management accounting for the Economic and Social Research Council (ESRC – at that time, SSRC). My objective in writing that paper was to survey the development of management accounting in the academic literature over the preceding twenty years or so in an attempt to assess the current state-of-the-art. The paper reviewed contemporary developments in management accounting research in quite broad terms and when I decided to use the general themes of the survey in my undergraduate teaching, I found it necessary to give students a number of lectures to introduce them to the concepts and techniques which have been discussed in the research literature. This book has arisen out of these lectures.

Readers who are familiar with the management accounting research literature are urged to read the survey paper, which has now been published along with two other ESRC-commissioned surveys in *Management Accounting, Organizational Theory and Capital Budgeting* by R. W. Scapens, D. T. Otley and R. J. Lister (Macmillan/ESRC, 1984). This present book is intended for readers who have not explored the research literature in any depth, but have some knowledge of standard textbook treatments of the subject. The contents of the book are aimed at second/third year students of management accounting and others who want to understand the directions of contemporary management accounting research.

It is assumed that the reader has had at least an introductory course in management accounting and is familiar with the topics typically covered in introductory textbooks. But a reader who has studied or is currently studying an intermediate management accounting textbook will also find this book very relevant. An attempt has been made to limit the complexity of highly mathematical topics – where mathematics are used they are kept as simple as possible and the interested reader is referred to more detailed treatments elsewhere. In general, emphasis is given to the interpretations and conclusions which can be drawn from mathematical analyses, rather than to the form of the analyses themselves.

No attempt is made to achieve a comprehensive coverage of all research which can be described as being within the field of management accounting. Certain important topic areas have been selected to illustrate the general nature of contemporary developments in management accounting research. Having completed the book, the reader should have an understanding of current academic thought in management accounting, a knowledge of where it has come from, and some ideas as to where it might lead.

I would like to express my gratitude to the ESRC for commissioning the survey paper which has led eventually to this book. In addition, my thanks are due to Professor Mike Bromwich, who first suggested that I should expand my survey paper into a book, and whose comments, criticisms and advice in the editorial process have contributed greatly to the end result. Mention should also be made of a number of my students who offered critical comments on earlier drafts. Finally, I would like to express my special thanks to my wife, Maureen, for her support and encouragement and for the many hours she spent word processing the material for this book.

December 1984   Robert W. Scapens

Preface to the Second Edition

In the five years since the first edition was published management accounting research has received considerable attention, particularly in the professional literature. The claims of Professors Johnson and Kaplan that management accounting has lost its relevance in the modern technological environment and is failing to give managers the information they need to compete in highly competitive world markets has created an atmosphere of crisis in management accounting circles. In this second edition these claims are discussed and a proposal to introduce a new system of cost accounting, called activity-based costing, is evaluated. In addition, reviews of other areas of accounting research are brought up to date.

The descriptions of management accounting practice in Chapter 3 have been extended to encompass the various case studies which have been published in recent years. But the major changes have been in Part IV, Current and Future Developments (Chapters 10–13), which has been revised and extended to include the developments which have taken place over the last five years. Chapter 10 (Agency Theory and Management Accounting) and Chapter 11 (Cost Allocation Models) have been revised and their order reversed. Chapter 12 is a new chapter which describes activity-based costing and Chapter 13 (previously Chapter 12) has been extended to evaluate the crisis in management accounting.

Other parts of the book are substantially unchanged, although amendments have been made in response to suggestions made by users of the first edition. In particular, I am grateful for comments received from my own students and from John Benzies, who read the first edition on to tape for the RNIB Student Tape Library. I would also like to thank my colleagues Trevor Hopper and Linda Lewis for commenting on the new material for the second edition. Finally, I want to thank again my wife, Maureen, for her continuing support and for her word processing.

June 1990   Robert W. Scapens

Management Accounting: Theory and Practice

Introduction 1

Over the past forty years management accounting has developed
as a practical aid to business managers and as a subject for
academic teaching and research. But now some writers are claim-
ing that management accounting is not relevant to the needs of the
managers of modern businesses. Management accounting textbooks written by academics describe a coherent set of concepts
and techniques which are available to management accountants in
practice. Unfortunately, in a number of respects, the practical
nature of the subject differs quite considerably from these textbook concepts and techniques. It could be said that there is a gap
between the 'theory' and 'practice' of management accounting – a
gap which is quite wide, particularly when 'theory' includes the
various mathematical and statistical techniques available for financial decision making – for example, linear programming and
statistical decision theory. However, contemporary developments
in management accounting research have provided a basis for
understanding the usefulness of textbook concepts and techniques.
This book reviews these contemporary developments.

A survey of management accounting textbooks (described in
Chapter 2) indicates a considerable measure of agreement
amongst textbook writers as to the nature of management account-

ing. The contents of those textbooks will be regarded, for purposes of this book, as indicative of the conventional wisdom of management accounting. In general, textbook writers give the impression that the conventional wisdom can provide the 'right answers', while practices which are inconsistent with it are in some sense wrong. Some of the examples and exercises in textbooks illustrate this latter point. For instance, an exercise which invites criticism of an absorption costing report 'prepared by the accountant' implies that the practising accountant is wrong, while the academic textbook writer can provide the 'correct answer'.

Over the past twenty years researchers have relaxed a number of the assumptions which are implied in management accounting's conventional wisdom. In particular, such researchers have explored the effects of uncertainty, information costs, and the motivations of managers/decision makers on the design and selection of appropriate management accounting techniques. This book reviews the work of these researchers. As well as giving the reader an awareness of current thinking in management accounting research, this review will place the apparent gap between the theory and practice of management accounting into perspective and provide a basis for evaluating the usefulness of the concepts and techniques contained in most current textbooks.

However, this book is not a textbook – no attempt is made at comprehensive coverage of management accounting. But with the aid of illustrations drawn from a number of representative areas, we will discuss contemporary developments in the subject. In order to discuss these developments in their proper context, subsequent chapters will trace the historical development of management accounting research.

In Chapter 2 the nature of the conventional wisdom of management accounting will be described and its origins explored. In particular, the underlying assumptions which were generally accepted (either implicitly or explicitly) by the researchers who developed the basic concepts and techniques will be identified. Emphasis will be given to the user decision approach which is common to most current management accounting textbooks. Such textbooks generally rely on simple economic models which embody the assumptions of profit maximisation and costless information. Much of the research which underlies management accounting's conventional wisdom was undertaken in the 1950s and early 1960s, particularly in the United States; but there were some notable contributions from the United Kingdom as early as the 1930s. No special attempt will be made to identify the geographical origins of particular theoretical developments. The limited extent to which this conventional wisdom is applied in practice will be discussed in Chapter 3. It will be argued that the gap between the conventional wisdom and the practice of management accounting is partly due to the nature of the assumptions used in the research which underlies the conventional wisdom.

As indicated above, much of this research was completed by the 1960s. Subsequent research, particularly in the early 1970s, attempted to remove some of the assumptions implied in the earlier work; for instance, the assumptions concerning certainty about the future. Researchers attempted to extend models for cost estimation, cost-volume-profit analysis and cost variance investigation to explicitly recognise uncertainty. These three areas will be discussed in Chapters 4, 5 and 6. Other areas were researched, but these three are described in this book as illustrations of the general trend. Such research led to models which were mathematically very complex and which have not been widely used in practice. It will be argued later in the book that the major problems with these complex models are that they fail to recognise the implementation problems and, more importantly, ignore the cost of information.

Information costs will be explicitly examined in Chapters 7 and 8, and some of the implications thereof will be explored in Chapter 9. These three chapters will discuss information economics, which became popular in management accounting research in the mid-1970s, and led to the realisation that when costs and benefits of information are taken into consideration, simple models can be rational. A decision maker faced with a complex situation may be quite rational to select a rule-of-thumb, if the costs of providing a more sophisticated solution outweigh the benefit to be derived therefrom. Chapter 9 will describe some empirical and stimulation studies which demonstrate such a result.

The last section of the book attempts to bring up to date this review of contemporary developments in management accounting research by looking at areas of research in the 1980s. Chapter 10 contains a discussion of the implications of agency theory – an extension of information economics. Using agency theory it is possible to demonstrate that some of the observed practices of management accounting could be optimal, despite their lack of conformity with conventional wisdom. Thus, agency theory may offer a means of closing the gap between the theory and practice of management accounting. But at the present time, agency theory provides few conclusions which can be generalised and empirically tested – most of the results of agency theory are situation specific, i.e., they describe the optimal techniques for particular situations.

One area of management accounting practice which is currently generating considerable debate is the allocation of overhead costs. This area will be discussed in general terms in Chapter 11, while Chapter 12 will describe activity-based costing which is a new technique designed to overcome the problems surrounding more conventional cost allocation techniques.

As already noted, this book is not a comprehensive textbook of management accounting. It does not deal with all the techniques which are contained within most textbooks. Furthermore, it retains the economic perspective of management accounting's conventional wisdom. Developments in behavioural accounting are not explicitly reviewed, although some references are made to them. A review of contemporary developments in behavioural accounting is left to other writers (e.g., Otley, 1984; and Emmanuel and Otley, 1985). It is hoped that the theme set up by examining the illustrative areas included in this book will provide an insight into current economic-based management accounting research and thereby enable the reader to take a more critical view of material contained in management accounting textbooks.

The Conventional Wisdom

The existence of a gap between the theory and practice of management accounting was suggested in Chapter 1. For this purpose the 'theory' or conventional wisdom of management accounting was equated with the contents of current textbooks. In this chapter an overview of the conventional wisdom will be provided and its underlying assumptions explored. It will be argued that there is a measure of agreement amongst textbook writers as to what comprises the core material or conventional wisdom, and that this conventional wisdom derives from research undertaken primarily in the 1950s and early 1960s. Students of management accounting should be quite familiar with this core material as it typically forms the basis of management accounting courses.

2.1 The Rise of Management Accounting

In its simplest terms, the conventional view is that management accounting comprises that branch of accounting which seeks to meet the needs of managers – or in general, the needs of users internal to the business. Thus, it could be said that management

7

accounting was first practised when businessmen began to receive financial information about their businesses. However, general use of the term management accounting (and its North American equivalent, managerial accounting) is comparatively new.

Before the Second World War the primary focus of internal accounting was the determination of costs, with particular emphasis on product costing and the control of direct labour, direct materials and overheads. Most of the innovators were cost accounting practitioners. The major concerns of cost accounting included the double-entry recording systems for cost control and the identification of unit costs – i.e., the cost for each product or departmental unit. Attempts were made to identify what could be considered the 'full' cost of producing each unit of output. These concerns led to various methods of cost identification and allocation, and to an emphasis on absorption costing.

After the Second World War there was an increasing awareness of the view that cost information, in particular, and accounting information, in general, should be appropriate to the needs of users – especially managers. In the academic field, a study by Simon *et al.* in 1954 had a profound effect on the perceived role of accounting information for managers. That study identified three uses of accounting information which managers considered important: score-card, attention-directing and problem-solving – all concerned with aspects of the management of organisational performance. This management process can be divided into two elements, planning and control. Management accounting developed as it became recognised that accounting information could be widely used in both managerial planning and managerial control.

A useful distinction between the era of cost accounting and the era of management accounting was made by Horngren:

In an exaggerated sense, the cost accountant's main mission might have been depicted as the pursuit of *absolute truth*, where truth was defined in terms of getting as accurate or precise costs as possible. . . . [While in management accounting] the theme of 'different costs for different purposes' was stressed – a preoccupation with finding *conditional truth*. (1975, pp. 9–10; emphasis added)

This change in the perceived nature of the internal accounting function was explicitly recognised by the professional accounting organisations. The Institute of Cost and Works Accountants changed the name of its journal from *Cost Accounting* to *Management Accounting* in 1965 and its own name to the Institute of Cost and Management Accountants in 1972. In the United States the National Association of Cost Accountants had changed its name to the National Association of Accountants in 1958.

The management accounting literature expanded rapidly in the 1960s as researchers first developed, and then refined, new techniques for providing accounting information to management. However, these techniques were developed on an *ad hoc* basis; there was no explicit statement of the underlying theory of management accounting which was used to guide this research. Nevertheless, it is possible to identify some of the assumptions which were implicit in the research and this will be attempted below.

At this stage it would be useful to provide a definition of management accounting, which could be used to structure the present discussion. Unfortunately, this is not an easy task as there is no generally agreed definition. Various definitions are available; but some are too general to provide a suitable structure, while others simply emphasise a particular research approach.

The professional management accounting bodies in the UK and US define management accounting in very general terms. Cox (1982), echoing the official view of the Institute of Cost and Management Accountants, argued that management accounting should not be restricted to internal reporting – see also National Association of Accountants (1981). The professional view appears to be that management accountants should be concerned with all aspects of accounting, except the external audit. This wide ranging view of management accounting includes the preparation of financial statements and the general financial management of the organisation within the management accounting function. While such a definition of management accounting might be appropriate from a professional perspective it does not provide a means of structuring a study of the subject.

Traditionally, the subject matter of accounting has been divided into sections, such as financial accounting and management accounting, for purposes of teaching, research and professional examinations. Undoubtedly, the sections overlap in practice, and the boundaries of each section can be described as arbitrary. However, the present discussion would be totally unmanageable in the absence of such boundaries. Rather than attempting to provide *a priori* justifications for the boundaries used in this book, the field of management accounting will be identified through an examination of management accounting textbooks. This will provide an indication of the core or conventional wisdom of management accounting as it is understood by academic textbook writers and presumably also by teachers of management accounting.

2.2   The Scope of Management Accounting

In 1982 a sample of 24 management accounting textbooks was used to identify the perceived scope of management accounting. No special selection techniques were used, just the books readily to hand. It has to be acknowledged that the availability of these books introduced a particular bias into the sample. Nevertheless, the facts that the textbook market is capable of sustaining such a large number of books and that similar books have continued to be published throughout the 1980s suggest that the bias is likely to be shared by a substantial number of accounting teachers. The material included in these textbooks indicates the aspects of management accounting currently being conveyed to accounting students – many of whom will become the next generation of management accounting practitioners.

As it appears that the terms cost accounting and management accounting now tend to be used synonymously in textbook titles, books with the words 'cost' or 'cost accounting' in the title were included in the sample. In a few cases, books with cost accounting titles included additional discussion of cost accounting systems, but in general there was a remarkable consensus in the material covered. A summary of the material is presented in Table 2.1. Several books included separate chapters dealing with quantitative aspects of management accounting and a few had chapters on behavioural aspects. Some books, notably Amey and Eggington (1973), Dopuch, Birnberg and Demski (1982) and Kaplan and Atkinson (1989), attempted to integrate such material into appropriate sections of the text. The only major change in the contents of books published in the second half of the 1980s has been the inclusion of some discussion of the implications of modern manufacturing techniques – for examples see Horngren and Foster (1987) and Kaplan and Atkinson (1989).

Some textbook writers include in management accounting such financial management topics as capital investment appraisal and working capital management. However, to avoid expanding the material in this book unnecessarily such topics will not be discussed in detail, although some references will be made to them in order to illustrate certain parallel developments in the field of financial management.

TABLE 2.1
Major Topics in the Field of Management Accounting

1 Planning	Relevant costs for decisions
	Cost–volume–profit analysis
	Product mix decisions
	Other decisions: e.g. economic order quantities
2 Cost classifications	Fixed and variable costs
	Cost estimation techniques
	Forecasting costs
	Learning curves
3 Control	Responsibility accounting
	Budgeting and standard costing
	Variance analysis
4 Costing	Job order and process costing
	Variable and absorption costing
	Cost allocation (including service department costs)
5 Divisionalised organisations	Performance evaluation
	Transfer pricing

An examination of pre-1980 editions of several management accounting textbooks suggests that the core material has not changed substantially during recent decades. Although modern manufacturing techniques have had some impact on textbooks published recently, the only major change in the material has been a decline in the space devoted to descriptions of cost accounting systems, particularly in textbooks with a cost accounting title. It is possible that teachers of management accounting at universities and elsewhere, especially in the UK, do not rely entirely on textbooks in designing their courses. But a survey in the early 1980s of seventeen universities and nine polytechnics in the UK suggested that a list of topics taken from Horngren (1977) provided an adequate basis for indicating the material covered in management accounting courses (Perks and Morrell, 1981). Furthermore, such textbooks appear prominently in the reading lists for the examinations of professional accounting bodies. Thus, it seems reasonable to assume that textbooks provide a satisfactory indication of the core material of management accounting.

Much of the material in Table 2.1 can be identified with research undertaken in the 1950s and 1960s. Each of the major topics is briefly discussed below and related to management accounting research up to approximately 1970. As will be seen this research provided the basis for the concepts and techniques which comprise management accounting's conventional wisdom. It will be assumed that the reader is reasonably familiar with this material, and so individual topics will not be described in detail. Rather, the origins of the material and its assumptions will be explored. In later chapters, however, the subsequent literature will be discussed rather more fully.

2.3   Planning

As indicated above, the impetus for the development of management accounting came with the acceptance of the view that accounting information should be appropriate for the needs of users. In particular, it was recognised that a single concept of cost could not be appropriate for all purposes. The phrase 'different costs for different purposes' became fundamental to the analysis of short-term planning, and indeed for management accounting in general. This phrase is generally associated with the somewhat earlier work of a US economist, J. Maurice Clark, who, in 1923, took a close look at cost accounting and argued that there can be no unique concept of cost. Similar ideas were developed in the UK, in particular at the London School of Economics, by economists and by accountants trained in economics. These economists argued that relevant costs can only be identified in the context of the particular decision being considered.

In much of the management accounting literature of the 1960s, and also in many current textbooks, the notion of different costs for different purposes is developed within a framework which relies on the assumption that decision makers are profit maximisers. For this purpose, the profit maximising objective is expressed in terms of marginal economic analysis, which gives rise to an incremental cash flow approach to decision making. The economic framework also assumes that the decision maker has available, at no cost, all the information needed to arrive at a deterministic solution to his/her choice problem. Most of the quantitative techniques developed in the 1960s are set within such a decision framework – as will be seen in the following discussion.

It is worth pointing out that the marginalist economic theories were never intended (at least by the economists) to serve as normative theories of how managers ought to behave. They were only meant to generate testable hypotheses about the economic activities of firms in aggregate. It was accountants who gave the theories their normative status. A major attraction of the economic framework (and the profit maximisation objective) was that it permitted a rigorous mathematical analysis of management accounting problems. This provided a considerable measure of academic respectability for the study of management accounting. But it has also meant that on occasions mathematical elegance has taken precedence over practical usefulness. Many of the mathematical models developed by academics are not used in practice – this issue is explored later.

An early use of mathematical analysis in management (and also in cost) accounting was in the study of break-even points. Simple break-even charts are described in many current management accounting textbooks along with discussions of the more general 'Cost–Volume–Profit' (C–V–P) analysis. Some writers have attempted to extend the analysis to the non-linear functions favoured by economists, but linear functions are generally retained for accounting applications.

Two major extensions of C–V–P analysis have been widely discussed in the management accounting literature: (1) uncertainty concerning the model's parameters, and (2) production limitations due to scarce resources. Jaedicke and Robichek (1964) wrote a seminal paper which explored the effects on C–V–P analysis of allowing uncertainty concerning certain parameters, such as sales volume. This represented a first step away from the conventional deterministic economic framework. Such treatments of uncertainty were not a common feature of management accounting research in the 1960s; nor are they extensively discussed in current management accounting textbooks, although textbook writers are now beginning to make reference to the nature of decision making under uncertainty and some writers of advanced textbooks (such as Kaplan and Atkinson, 1989) discuss the subject at some length. Further discussion is deferred to Chapter 5.

Jaedicke was also an important contributor to the second major extension of C–V–P analysis, i.e., for a multiproduct firm with numerous production constraints (see Jaedicke, 1961). He demonstrated that an optimal product mix can be determined by linear programming. By the end of the decade the simple linear break-even model had been extended to cover multiple products and multiple constraints. According to Kaplan (1977, p. 35):

> **This progression . . . highlighted the key feature of the product mix decision – maximizing contribution margin per unit of scarce resource consumed – and demonstrated that departures from the simple linear assumptions can be handled relatively easily within the mathematical programming framework.**

Some discussion of linear programming is now included in most management accounting textbooks.

These developments took place as a result of, and sometimes alongside, advances in the field of operational research (OR). However, the boundary between management accounting and OR was unclear. It has been suggested that the role of management accounting should be to provide: (1) information for the model builder, (2) data for the model, and (3) monitoring of decision outcomes (Hartley, 1968). The development of linear programming decision models could be regarded as operational research, while the provision of information for their development or application could be regarded as the province of management accounting.

Advances in the field of OR were important for management accounting research in the 1960s, and a number of OR models were applied in accounting contexts. Such models were frequently at the centre of the user-decision approach. Typically, the models applied in management accounting assumed that the decision maker wishes to maximise contribution and has available the necessary information to arrive at a deterministic solution, i.e., they adopted the economic framework, described earlier.

2.4 Cost Classifications

The classification of costs as direct or indirect, fixed or variable, period or product, and so on was useful for cost accounting, but became particularly important with the development of management accounting. The recognition that different cost concepts are needed for different purposes (discussed above) gave a new emphasis to cost classifications.

Current management accounting textbooks give particular attention to the classification of costs as fixed or variable. This reflects the short-run decision-making orientation of much current management accounting thought. Long-run incremental cost concepts are sometimes included in discussions of relevant costs for decisions, but generally the decision situations involve fixed capacity. In such cases, the distinction between fixed and variable costs is particularly important. This is clearly seen in the product mix decisions and C–V–P analysis described earlier.

Statistical regression techniques are frequently portrayed as the preferred methods for classifying costs into their fixed and variable elements. However, there are few empirical studies describing the actual use of regression analysis for cost classification. Scatter graphs appear to have been the only technique widely used in practice in the 1960s (National Association of Accountants, 1960), but it was argued by certain writers that regression techniques are superior (Gynther, 1963; McClenon, 1963; and Raun, 1964). The advantages and difficulties of such techniques are described in Chapter 4.

In some textbooks the use of regression analysis for predicting costs and revenues is briefly discussed and occasionally alternative forecasting techniques are mentioned, e.g., time series analysis and exponential smoothing. But in general the decision maker is assumed to have available all the information he/she requires. For instance, if total costs are a function of the units sold it would be assumed that production and sales forecasts are available. This information may be provided by specialists in other fields, such as production engineering and statistics, which are considered to be outside the scope of management accounting. The choice of alternative information sources is not explicitly considered. This is consistent with an economic framework which does not address problems of information acquisition.

The *raison d'être* of cost classification and estimation is the provision of information for the decision maker. The techniques described above derive from the notion of different costs for different purposes, and have a short-run decision orientation. Considerable attention is given to the separation of fixed and variable elements of total costs. The usefulness of this classification, however, is not restricted to planning, it also has relevance in the control process discussed below.

2.5   Control

Management accounting, as found in current textbooks, places the notion of responsibility accounting at the very centre of the management control system. The techniques practised in the name of responsibility accounting are many and varied. In an attempt to pin down the nature of responsibility accounting Ferrara's definition will be used.

> **The essence of responsibility accounting is the accumulation of cost and revenues according to areas of responsibility in order that deviations from standard costs and budgets can be identified with the person or group responsible.** (1964, p. 11)

Although standard costing and budgetary control had been developed in the early decades of the twentieth century it was in the late 1950s and early 1960s that responsibility accounting developed rapidly in the vanguard of advances in management accounting. Its development and popularity were major steps in the movement from cost control to managerial control which typified the emergence of management accounting. The conventional wisdom relating to responsibility accounting is that accounting reports should distinguish elements of performance which are controllable by the recipient of the report from those elements which are uncontrollable.

Responsibility accounting conforms to the classical principles of management which emphasise lines of authority and responsibility. These principles had a substantial impact on organisational design in the 1950s, and it was argued that the responsibility accounting system should be founded upon the company's organisation structure. Initially the motivational role of responsibility accounting was not well understood. But when behavioural theories entered the management accounting literature it was recognised that responsibility accounting could have motivational consequences. Despite this recognition of behavioural research many of the techniques offered in the name of responsibility accounting (in current textbooks) do not fully reflect advances in that field.

The use of standard costs and/or budgets to quantify plans (or targets) for responsibility centres, and the measurement of performance in terms of variances therefrom, is the primary method of managerial control described in current management accounting textbooks. Budgetary control and standard costing, however, pre-date quite considerably the notion of responsibility accounting. It is the emphasis given to them and the calculation of variances for each responsibility centre which characterises the modern use of these techniques for responsibility accounting.

With the recognition of a need for information for managerial control, traditional methods of calculating variances were criticised for failing to provide relevant information to managers and alternatives were proposed. These alternatives were derived from the economic framework that was used in analysing decision-making situations.

At the simplest level the development of marginal cost and contribution approaches to decision making led to an emphasis in the literature on marginal standard costing, in contrast to the full (absorption) costing approach common in the earlier forms of standard costing. Many textbook writers appear to have a preference for the contribution approach (although full costing is still widely used in practice – see Chapter 3). The tangible effects of this preference can be seen in computations of sales and overhead variances. It is argued that sales variances should be measured in terms of contribution margins and that overhead variances should reflect the distinction between fixed and variable costs.

At a more fundamental level attempts have been made to integrate the new management accounting approaches to planning explicitly into the accounting control system. Samuels (1965) was probably the first to relate a linear programming formulation of the typical product-mix decision problem to the calculation of variances. He suggested that dual prices on scarce resources could be charged to production departments and variances computed in terms of opportunity losses. These opportunity loss variances were an attempt to assess the difference between the actual outcome and the best achievable plan. Although the proposed system had defects, it has been recognised as the first attempt at integrating control systems and formal decision models.

In a seminal paper, Dopuch *et al.* (1967) argued that an extension of variance analysis to the evaluation of the outcomes of formal decision models would require changes in both the types of variances calculated and the methods used for assessing their significance. Their analysis of economic order quantities and product mix models introduced the notion of opportunity loss variances. Demski (1967) provided an illustration of such variances using *ex post* analysis. He suggested that an opportunity loss variance could be computed by comparing actual performance against an *ex post* optimum, i.e., the best performance which should have been possible given the actual environmental conditions. Some of the assumptions of his analysis have been questioned, but the idea of opportunity loss variances seems to have been widely accepted, although not extensively integrated into current textbooks.

The paper by Dopuch *et al.* (1967) led to another major development in the literature – variance investigation models.

Standard cost systems generate a vast number of variances each period. If the standard cost system is to be effective the variances which are most significant should be investigated to determine their source and to correct the process if possible. But how should variances be selected for investigation? Essentially this is a decision problem which is no different from those discussed earlier. Statistical control procedures were adapted and operational research-type models were developed. Although these later models were further discussed in the 1970s, only the simplest models are described in current textbooks, and these are in general deterministic profit-maximising models. Models for variance investigation decisions will be discussed in Chapter 6.

Although considerable behavioural research has been undertaken in the area of budgeting and standard costing, it has had a very limited impact on the techniques which are offered in current management accounting textbooks. A number of behavioural researchers explored the relationship between behavioural science and management accounting in the 1960s. Some management accounting textbooks now include at least a chapter on 'behavioural implications', but only in so far as they affect the setting of standards, the agreement of budgets and the uses of variance reports. In addition, there are a number of specialist behavioural accounting textbooks. Nevertheless, the effects of behavioural research on the techniques which can be regarded as basic to management accounting's conventional wisdom have been minimal. This is surprising in view of the fact that the economic framework which underlies these techniques is inconsistent with much modern behavioural research, and that economists have developed behavioural theories of the firm, e.g., Cyert and March (1963) and alternative models of decision making, e.g., Simon (1960).

2.6 Costing

The amount of material on costing methods in management accounting textbooks has been declining over the years. However, costing methods have recently become a source of considerable debate, especially in the professional literature, with claims that the methods of allocating overheads which are widely used in practice are distorting production costs and undermining industrial competitiveness. This debate, which as yet has had only a limited impact on management accounting textbooks, will be discussed later. Most current textbooks discuss briefly the nature of job-order and (sometimes) process costing systems, the distinction between variable and absorption costing, and cost allocations.

Job-order and process costing are normally used to illustrate cost-accumulation systems and to provide an introduction to cost allocations. Although the basic principles for these systems belong to an era of cost accounting when manufacturing processes were typically rather different from those of today, there have been some subsequent studies.

The distinction between marginal (or variable) costing and absorption costing was mentioned earlier, where it was indicated that many management accounting textbook writers appear to favour the marginal costing approach. The comparison with absorption costing is usually included in textbooks for two reasons. First, it demonstrates the advantages of marginal costing and the distortions introduced by absorption costing. Second, as absorption costing is widely used to value inventories for the published financial statements, it provides the means for reconciling financial and management accounts.

Although the origins of cost allocations belong to the era of cost accounting, a considerable literature built up in the 1960s (and to a lesser extent in the 1970s) using mathematical methods for cost allocations. Some writers argued that all such allocations are arbitrary (see Thomas, 1969; 1980). Indeed, some contributors to the literature began their papers by agreeing with Thomas. They then pointed out that as cost allocations are observed in practice preferred methods should be identified, e.g., Moriarity (1975). Linear programming and matrix algebra became a feature of this literature in the 1960s and are mentioned in most current textbooks.

Whilst some of this literature is inconsistent with the management decision approach of management accounting (and acknowledged to be so) there are connections with the economic framework described earlier. The mathematical programming methods for allocating joint cost, for instance, follow suggestions in the economic literature (based on marginalist principles) that in certain circumstances such allocations can provide relevant costs for decision making. An important prerequisite for many of the allocation methods developed over the years is that they do not distort the decisions which would be made without such allocations. The current debate about methods of cost allocation will be outlined in Chapter 3 and discussed further in Chapters 11 and 12.

2.7 Divisionalised Organisations

It is customary for management accounting textbooks to include at least one chapter dealing with the special problems of divisionalised organisations. However, no new principles are involved. Divisional performance measurement is an application of the notion of responsibility accounting discussed earlier and transfer pricing can be considered a special form of cost allocation.

Return on investment as a measure of divisional performance gained much popularity after the Second World War, but various problems were identified and some refinements were suggested. Solomons (1965) proposed the use of residual income, i.e., profit less a notional interest charge computed by reference to divisional capital employed. This proposal appears to have received the support of many textbooks especially in the United States, although some remain unconvinced (Shillinglaw, 1977) and some are against the proposal (e.g., Amey and Eggington, 1973).

As an alternative to using return on investment or residual income some writers have suggested assessing divisional performance against budgets. Such proposals put this topic firmly back into the earlier discussion of responsibility accounting and budgetary control. Amey (1969) proposed that the divisional budgets should be derived from the solution to the group's linear programming problem. This is a further extension of the idea advanced by Samuels (1965) and is related to the use of linear programming for setting transfer prices.

Much of the early analysis of the transfer pricing problem was undertaken by economists, although some accountants were also interested in the area. An important consideration in the development of transfer prices was that divisional decision makers should be motivated to select courses of action which maximise the profits of the organisation as a whole. Transfer prices based on the dual values (or shadow prices) derived from a linear programming problem of the group as a whole were offered as a means of ensuring congruence between divisional and group objectives. This approach requires the centralisation of planning, and could defeat the benefits of divisionalisation. From this perspective transfer prices can be viewed as a means of contriving divisional decisions to maximise group profits. Thus transfer pricing can be fitted into the decision-making framework discussed earlier in this chapter.

2.8 Some Implied Assumptions of Management Accounting

It is hoped that the reader has recognised in the preceding discussion the essential elements of management accounting, as it is currently taught at many universities and colleges in the United Kingdom, North America and many other parts of the world. The particular topics included in this discussion could be criticised for various reasons – for instance, some may argue that the boundaries of management accounting were drawn too narrowly, while others may argue that the focus on particular techniques was inappropriate. All that has been attempted is a review of the major topics which are sufficiently accepted to be included in current textbooks. No particular definition of management accounting was adopted.

The material discussed above was oriented towards the manufacturing function, as this is the primary focus of most textbooks (and of much management accounting research). This has meant that the distribution and marketing functions have not been explicitly mentioned. However, similar general principles might be applied to these functions, although research in these areas is limited.

The term 'conditional truth' was used to depict the general theme of management accounting, and to distinguish it from the 'absolute truth' theme of cost accounting. The notion of 'conditional truth' is appropriate because management accounting, as described above, implies that different costs are needed for different purposes, or in other words, accounting information depends on the information needs of managers. Thus, in developing management accounting concepts and techniques researchers had to identify managers' information needs. In general, this meant constructing decision models to indicate how decisions are, or should be, made. Once the decision model is postulated the conditional truth approach implies that the appropriate information can be determined by deductive reasoning, i.e., truth can be attained.

It was indicated earlier that an economic framework played a central role in structuring the decision models used by the researchers who were instrumental in the development of management accounting's conventional wisdom. It is not suggested that economics was the only influence. Other disciplines, such as management science, organisation theory and, latterly, behavioural science have undoubtedly had an influence, but economics and especially the marginalist principles of neo-classical economics, probably had the dominant influence. This economic approach entails the following assumptions. The decision maker has available, at no cost and without uncertainty, all the information he/she requires to completely structure the decision problem and to arrive at a deterministic profit maximising solution, using the principles of marginal analysis.

In management accounting decision models, profit maximisation is expressed in terms of profits accruing to the owners of the business. This implies a further assumption that the decision maker either is the owner or shares the owner's goals for the business. Where the decision makers are not the owners, management accounting relies on the techniques of responsibility accounting to achieve goal congruence. In the early days of management accounting, the way in which such techniques achieved goal congruence was unclear. More recently, research in the field of organisational behaviour has provided some insights. Nevertheless, it is still assumed that the decision maker is a profit maximiser. This is not to suggest that profit maximisation is necessarily an appropriate description of decision making in practice. Rather, it is simply an assumption of the decision models which underlie the conventional wisdom of management accounting.

A further implied assumption of management accounting decision models is that individual decision makers can be isolated from other decision makers within the organisation. This can be seen in that decision makers are identified as individuals, and group decision making is not considered. Group decisions are ignored because they are a trivial extension of individual decisions within the economic framework. All decision makers are assumed to be profit maximisers and complete and perfect information assumptions provide a common information set. As a result, every decision maker within this framework will arrive at the same decisions, and so any one of them can be analysed independently.

The complete and perfect information assumptions permit unlimited mathematical sophistication in quantitative techniques. Decision makers are assumed to have the knowledge to use any mathematical techniques and costless information processing places no limits on the complexity of the information system. Once such a decision is analysed the appropriate accounting information can be determined.

The costs of providing such information in the real world and the uncertainty involved in all practical decision making are only discussed in the most general terms in current management accounting textbooks. It is generally implied that information costs and uncertainty are outside the realm of management accounting techniques and must be handled by management intuition! Demski and Feltham, in a brief review of the conditional truth theme, identified three fundamental defects of management accounting which provide a useful summary of the above discussion:

> **First, truth – even if desirable – cannot be obtained without incurring a cost. Measurement consumes resources . . . Second, users operate in an uncertain world and explicit recognition of uncertainty casts doubt on the concept of a true cost, which implicitly presumes a certain world. . . . Third, the concept of a true cost (whether conditional or absolute) is likely to be both illusory and irrelevant in a multiperson world.** (1976, pp. 7–8)

As a response to these defects Demski and Feltham proposed an information economics approach (which will be described in Chapter 8). Although this approach abandons some elements of the economic framework described above, it keeps the study of management accounting firmly within the field of economics. As mentioned in Chapter 1, this book reviews contemporary developments in management accounting research from an economic perspective. Other perspectives, e.g., organisational and political, may provide alternative explanations of the practice of management accounting – but they are outside the scope of this book.

Before addressing such issues through a discussion of management accounting research, Chapter 3 will briefly examine management accounting in practice.

Management
Accounting
Practice

3

Chapter 2 attempted to demonstrate that many aspects of management accounting's conventional wisdom, as portrayed in current textbooks, can be seen in the research which took place in the 1950s and 1960s. Today, it is generally supposed that this research has had only a limited impact on practice. The purpose of this chapter is to explore published empirical evidence of management accounting practice.

3.1   The Gap Between Theory and Practice

The first edition of this book was written against the background of an increasing awareness, on the part of researchers in the UK, of a gap between the theory and practice of management accounting. Although, at that time, there was only limited evidence available, those studies which had been published did little to contradict the supposition that management accounting's conventional wisdom is not entirely compatible with management accounting practice.

For example, an examination of the management accounting practices of a small sample of 14 companies led researchers at the University of Aston to conclude that 'there appears to be a substantial gap between theory and practice' (Coates *et al.*, 1983). For this purpose they equated 'theory' with the conventional wisdom of management accounting discussed in Chapter 2.

In the day to day operation of management accounting systems, Coates *et al.* observed little formal analysis of cost behaviour, even though such analysis was considered to be important by some managers. Most of the sample companies operated absorption-based costing systems and there was little use of marginal cost analysis, although some managers claimed to know what their marginal costs were. The predominance of absorption-based costing in the UK has been supported by other studies. For instance, Finnie and Sizer (1983) found that all the companies in their sample of 22 engineering companies used absorption costing systems.

The conventional wisdom of management accounting textbooks suggests that absorption costing systems cannot provide relevant costs for all purposes. As an illustration, consider pricing decisions. In describing relevant costs for pricing, most accounting textbooks use a marginal cost approach. In another study, Scapens *et al.* (1983) observed that accounting information routinely provided for pricing decisions is normally based on absorption costing. Such information may not represent the relevant costs for such decisions, as no explicit recognition is made of opportunity costs. Only five of the 99 companies which were included in the Scapens *et al.* study made any use of the marginal cost approach in providing information to price setters. It has to be admitted, however, that although formal management accounting systems do not appear to follow the textbook prescriptions, decision makers (such as price setters) may, in practice, modify the accounting information they receive, such that their actions are in fact based upon the concepts implied in the conventional wisdom described in Chapter 2. However, as we will discuss in Chapter 12, it is now being argued that the use of conventional management accounting techniques is itself inappropriate for product pricing decisions.

Coates *et al.* observed a general lack of 'sophisticated' mathematical techniques in management accounting. They found no evidence of linear programming and other mathematical techniques for budget setting, transfer pricing or decision making. In another study, Gregory and Piper (1983) found little evidence of sophisticated techniques for stock control. Although many management accounting textbooks describe mathematical models for determining economic order quantities and stock levels, Gregory and Piper found only simple techniques being used in practice. That study and the others cited above gave support to the general view that UK companies tend not to use the various quantitative techniques advanced in the academic literature.

A number of similar studies have been published in North America, describing the use of various quantitative techniques in US industry. Although many of these studies were primarily concerned with the implementation of operational research and management science techniques, their results are of interest in the context of this chapter because the application of quantitative techniques is an important element of management accounting's conventional wisdom. Generally, these studies indicated that whilst some US companies do make use of quantitative techniques in areas such as long range planning and operations management, there are a large number of companies which do not make any extensive use of such techniques. Furthermore, it is the simpler techniques which tend to be preferred in most instances – see Green *et al.* (1977) for a list of such studies.

The application of quantitative techniques in US industry has increased only gradually over the years, even though one might expect techniques which offer a competitive advantage to be readily accepted in practice. In addition to the high cost of using many quantitative techniques (relative to the benefits which they generate) various barriers to their use have been identified. These barriers include the absence and/or unreliability of the required data, the inability of some users to understand complex techniques and the lack of time to apply them.

Ackoff has argued that the operational research function in US industry has been pushed down the organisation over the years because the techniques are of little value to senior corporate executives, although they may be useful for routine planning at lower managerial levels (1978, p. 4). Such a change is difficult to discern through questionnaire surveys of the type used in the studies described above. Generally, these studies only investigated whether or not certain quantitative techniques are used in the organisation, and not the point in the organisation at which they are used.

In the UK, Argenti (1976) asked, 'Whatever happened to management techniques?'. He pointed out that in the mid-1960s modern management techniques, including operational research, were regarded with great enthusiasm. A decade later, those techniques were apparently quite neglected by British industry. One response to Argenti's question was that some of the new techniques would be implemented after they had been fully tested. To Argenti it appeared that the 1970s were the era of simple techniques and that the more complex alternatives were unlikely to be implemented.

This brief discussion suggests that in the 1970s and early 1980's some simple quantitative techniques were used by companies in both the US and UK, but there was rather limited use of the more complex techniques. However, one study appeared to reach a different conclusion. Kiani-Aslani attempted to demonstrate that US management accountants do use the quantitative techniques set out in the textbooks (1977–8). His conclusion was that 96 per cent of company accountants in his sample of US companies – taken from the *Fortune 500* – used the quantitative methods taught in management accounting courses. However, included in his figure of 96 per cent were people who used the techniques only occasionally or rarely. Some of the techniques were used primarily for operations management, rather than in accounting applications. Thus, Kiani-Aslani's findings are not incompatible with the conclusions of the studies described earlier.

3.2 Management Accounting Case Studies

In the early years of the 1980s researchers tended to use questionnaire surveys in their studies of management accounting practice. But as the decade progressed greater attention was given to case studies – see Scapens *et al.* (1987) for some British case studies. These studies were attempts to understand the nature of management accounting practice and indirectly to explain the apparent gap between theory and practice which had been identified in the questionnaire studies. For instance, the researchers at the University of Aston followed up their questionnaire study with case studies based on face–to–face interviews (Coates *et al.*, 1987). Although their interviews did not directly contradict the evidence they had previously collected about the gap between theory and practice, they did observe managers using concepts such as fixed and variable costs, and techniques such as marginal costing – all central elements of management accounting's conventional wisdom. However, these concepts and techniques were used alongside more traditional practices, such as absorption costing.

Such observations suggest that the gap between theory and practice should be examined by studying both the extent and the context of the use of management accounting's conventional wisdom. Other studies, such as Berry *et al.* (1987) and Roberts and Scapens (1987), have attempted to describe management accounting in practice, with the objective of developing theories which explain management accounting in more complex terms than the simple economic model described in Chapter 2. For example, case studies have examined the way in which management accounting practices can be used to maintain the separate parts of a business as an organisational whole, despite the different vested interests and relative power of the various organisational participants.

In the US also, case studies have become an established method of researching management accounting practice. Interest in management acounting case studies was particularly stimulated in that country by the claims of Johnson and Kaplan that management accounting practice is not relevant for the needs of modern business enterprises. They argue that over the last forty years management accounting has come to be dominated by the requirements of external financial reporting and has, consequently, lost its relevance for managers.

In a historical review of 'The Rise and Fall of Management Accounting', Johnson and Kaplan (1987) observed that the techniques of management accounting were developed in the late nineteenth and early twentieth centuries through the practical innovations of entrepreneurs and businessmen; for example, through the work of scientific management engineers, such as Frederick Taylor who developed techniques for measuring physical and cost standards which were later to form the basis of standard costing systems. Furthermore, in the early decades of the twentieth century, the Du Pont Power Company developed return on investment (ROI) as a measure of the commercial success of operating units, and in the 1920s the company's chief financial officer, F. Donaldson Brown, decomposed ROI into its components parts – an operating return (return on sales) and asset turnover (sales to assets).

Such techniques are now widely used in practice. In fact, Johnson and Kaplan argue that virtually all management accounting practices in use today were in place by 1925 and that there have been few apparent changes in management accounting practices since then, despite the substantial changes which have taken place in manufacturing operations due to advances in technology.

Nevertheless, they believe that researchers should be looking for accounting innovations in modern-day businesses. In a discussion of research methods, Kaplan urged researchers to study the innovative practices of the successful companies in the late 20th century and to find 'the Pierre Du Ponts, Donaldson Browns, Alfred Sloans, and Frederick Taylors of the late 1980s'.

Such an approach presupposes that researchers can identify innovative practices and distinguish them, not only from common practices, but also from practices which might be in some way inferior. In other words, researchers need to have a clear understanding of the nature of management accounting practice in order to recognise certain practices as superior to others. Kaplan would probably respond that such questions can only be answered by the practitioners themselves. But any research which attempts to identify innovative (or 'best') practices will be influenced by the researcher's own conception of the nature of management accounting practice.

In general, Kaplan's writing suggests that he sees management accounting as the means by which senior management maintain control of the economic activities of their businesses and, in particular, the actions of their middle managers. The role of management accounting practice is taken for granted in the research process outlined by Kaplan, although there appears to be an underlying dependence on the conventional wisdom. It could be argued that Johnson and Kaplan's arguments are simply an elaboration of the view that there is a gap between the theory and practice of management accounting. As will be discussed in

Chapter 12, the research undertaken to date by Kaplan and his colleagues in the US has been particularly concerned with product costing in high-technology businesses.

Similar research has been undertaken in the UK, the primary contribution of which has been to increase the awareness of the nature of management accounting practice. In general, this research describes a view of practice which is rather different from management accounting's conventional wisdom. For example, Littler and Sweeting (1989) describe the flexible use which is made of accounting information in businesses using new production technologies. A similar view is presented by Innes and Mitchell (1989) in their study of accounting change in electronics companies.

In another study, Coates and Longden (1989) set out to identify new management accounting techniques which have been developed to cope with advances in technology. However, they found no new techniques. But they did find companies using new management accounting systems which rely extensively on advances in information technology. Although such systems make use of existing management accounting techniques, information technology allows the management accountant to provide 'better' information flows – in particular, information flows which provide information more quickly and which give more relevant information to managers. To understand the significance of these findings, they should be set alongside those of Littler and Sweeting, and Innes and Mitchell.

These three studies were commissioned by the Chartered Institute of Management Accountants to explore the effects on management accounting practices of advances in technology. Specifically, the researchers examined the following hypothesis: 'Growth businesses in high technology have adapted long-standing management accounting techniques, and have created new ones, to cope with the demands of the new product environment'. Taken together, the three studies show that it is not the particular management accounting techniques or procedures which have changed as a result of technological advances, but the uses made of the management accounting systems. For example, rather than regarding accounting information as a primary decision input which links action and outcomes, managers are now tending to focus on what they regard as the critical indicators, many of which are qualitative in nature. Furthermore, budgeting is seen as a process for facilitating dialogue and for exploring assumptions, rather than the primary financial control device.

Such research illustrates that accounting information, especially in conditions of rapid technological change, is partial and uncertain, and needs to be used with care and in a flexible manner alongside the other information which is available from both within and outside the business. However, there is little suggestion that new techniques are being developed, nor indeed is there any widespread application of the conventional wisdom contained in management accounting textbooks. Support is given to Johnson and Kaplan's claim that management accounting techniques have developed very little in recent years. Indeed, Coates and Longden (1989) suggest that developments in management accounting practices are often constrained by tradition and organisational inertia.

Thus, recent research has not changed the view taken in the first edition that the conventional wisdom is not entirely compatible with current practice. This casts considerable doubt on any suggestion that the reason for the gap between theory and practice is that it takes time for new ideas to become fully developed, accepted and implemented. Many of the textbook concepts and techniques have been advocated for several decades. Thus, it would seem reasonable to expect them to have been widely adopted if they offered any real benefits.

3.3 Explaining the Gap

It could be argued that the time lag between theory and practice should actually be quite short if the economic theory which underlies much of management accounting's conventional wisdom is appropriate. In a competitive economy, firms which do not adopt the best available techniques will be placed at a competitive disadvantage, relative to firms which do adopt such techniques. The forces of competition should ensure that new techniques of management accounting will be implemented quite quickly if they assist decision makers to maximise their profits: that is, if the marginal benefits exceed the marginal costs of their implementation. Thus, reasons other than the existence of a simple time lag are needed to explain the gap between the theory and practice of management accounting.

In view of the above economic arguments, the lack of acceptance of management accounting's conventional wisdom might be explained by one or both of the following: (1) the failure of the conventional wisdom to meet the needs of decision makers (for instance, because it is not relevant to the decision maker's needs or it is too costly to implement), or (2) the competitive economy assumptions which underlie management accounting's conventional wisdom are not appropriate to the circumstances of management accounting in practice. Both these explanations raise questions concerning the validity of the economic framework which was described in Chapter 2. Accordingly, it would seem reasonable to look for explanations of the gap between theory and practice by questioning the basis of the theory, as well as by exploring the nature of practice. In the following chapters of this book the basis of management accounting's conventional wisdom will be explored and the results of recent research will be used to put existing practice into context.

Chapters 4, 5 and 6 illustrate some extensions of the economic framework which was described in Chapter 2. These extensions, however, do not provide models and techniques which are particularly attractive to practitioners. Although the researchers looked at the complexity of decision making in the real world and sought to produce 'realistic' models, the techniques they produced frequently required too much information for their implementation in practice. In many cases, these researchers ignored the costs of providing such information. In Chapters 7, 8 and 9 further extensions which explicitly recognised the costs (and benefits) of information will be explored. It will be argued that the use of simple techniques in practice may in fact be an optimal response to the decision making situation and not an irrational rejection of 'academic' techniques – the benefits of using complex techniques may not outweigh the information costs which would be incurred.

The recognition by researchers that the use of simple techniques in practice may be quite rational led to a change of emphasis in management accounting research. During the 1980s, research became increasingly concerned with providing explanations of existing practice, rather than prescriptions of some notion of 'best' practice. Some of this research, in particular the research which uses agency theory to study management accounting, is discussed in Chapter 10. The recent resurgence of interest in cost accounting, however, has returned some accounting researchers to the search for 'best' practice. In Chapter 11 cost allocations will be discussed generally, and Chapter 12 will explore the current interest in activity-based costing. Finally, Chapter 13 will suggest some directions for the future.

Extension of Quantitative Models

Statistical Regression Analysis

As statistical regression analysis for cost estimation and forecasting was discussed in the management accounting literature in the mid-1960s, it could be considered part of the conventional wisdom of management accounting. However, the use of such statistical methods requires acceptance, at least implicitly, that costs and revenues are uncertain. Thus, it could be argued that the discussion of statistics in the management accounting literature represented a first step away from the certainty assumption of the economic model discussed in Chapter 2.

In this chapter regression analysis for cost estimation and forecasting will be explored using firstly a simple regression model, and subsequently a multiple regression model. The purpose of the chapter is to illustrate the use of regression analysis in management accounting. The discussion will focus on the use and interpretation of the statistics rather than on the underlying statistical methods. It will be assumed that the reader has some familiarity with the statistical concepts which underlie regression analysis. However, if the reader is prepared to accept the validity of the equations used, a lack of such familiarity should not hinder an understanding of the chapter.

The simple regression model specifies the relationship between two variables; X, which is referred to as the independent variable, and Y, which is referred to as the dependent variable. The relationship between these two variables is expressed in the form of the following linear equation:

$$Y = a + bX \tag{4.1}$$

This equation represents a causal model. It is assumed that the value of the dependent variable, Y, depends on the value of the independent variable, X. The value of X is determined outside the model, but once it is known a value for Y can be computed. The object of regression analysis is to estimate the values of a and b in equation (4.1). The statistical method involves using previously observed values for X and Y in order to obtain a best estimate of the 'parameters' a and b.

A multiple regression model is very similar, but involves two or more independent variables. Thus, the equation relating the dependent variable, Y, to the multiple independent variables, X_i (where $i = 1, ..., n$), can be expressed in the following form:

$$Y = a + b_1X_1 + b_2X_2 + ... + b_nX_n \tag{4.2}$$

In this case, the statistical method will provide estimates of the $(n+1)$ parameters $a, b_1, b_2, ..., b_n$.

In the following sections of this chapter, the use of both simple and multiple regression will be discussed in accounting contexts and some of the statistical problems which arise as a result of the particular nature of accounting contexts will be examined.

4.1 The Use of Regression Analysis

The above introductory comments indicated that regression analysis can be used for both forecasting and cost estimation. Some further comments on each of these uses are made below.

Forecasting

An estimated equation (in the form of either equation (4.1) or equation (4.2)) could be used to forecast the value of the dependent variable, Y, in some future period. This variable could be the total costs of the business or of some part thereof: a machine, a department, etc. If regression analysis has been used to determine the relationship between the dependent variable and the independent variable(s), the estimated equation can be used to forecast a value of the dependent variable given any particular value(s) for the independent variable(s). The dependent variable need not be expressed in terms of costs, however. The model could be used to forecast demand for a particular product, the availability of supplies, the amount sold by competitors and so on. Nevertheless, in the present context, attention will be given primarily to forecasting costs.

Cost estimation

The primary concerns of regression analysis for cost estimation are the parameters a and b in simple regression and a, b_1, b_2, ..., b_n in multiple regression. Consider simple regression. If Y represents total costs and X represents units produced, then it follows that a represents fixed costs of production, while b represents variable production costs per unit of output. In the case of multiple regression the a again represents fixed costs, while b_1, ..., b_n represent the variable costs.

Much of the discussion of regression analysis in the management accounting literature has been concerned with estimating fixed and variable costs. However, it is also relevant to explore the use of regression analysis for forecasting total costs (and other variables) as forecasts are an essential input to most decision models used in management accounting.

4.2 The Least Squares Regression Model

As mentioned above, the object of simple regression is to estimate the relationship between a dependent variable and an independent variable, expressed in the form of equation (4.1). The estimate is prepared on the basis of past observations of values on the dependent and independent variables. However, the independent variable may be unable to explain fully the variation in the dependent variable. Accordingly, an equation relating the dependent and independent variables should be written as follows:

$$Y = a + bX + e \qquad (4.3)$$

where e represents an 'error term', i.e., the variation in Y which is not explicable in terms of variation in X.

Regression analysis produces an estimate of the underlying equation; but expressed in the form:

$$\hat{Y} = \hat{a} + \hat{b}X \qquad (4.4)$$

where a 'hat' ($\wedge$) over a variable or a parameter denotes an estimate. Equation (4.4) can be used to estimate values for the dependent variable, $\hat{Y}$, using the estimated parameters, $\hat{a}$ and $\hat{b}$, and observed values of the independent variable. As equation (4.4) is only an estimate of equation (4.3), each estimate, $\hat{Y}_i$, is likely to differ from the observed value, Y_i.

The method of regression analysis attempts to minimise the square of such differences, i.e.:

$$\text{minimise} \ \sum_i \ (Y_i - \hat{Y}_i)^2 \qquad (4.5)$$

These differences are illustrated by dotted lines on Figure 4.1. It should be noted that it is the vertical distances which are mini-

FIGURE 4.1
A Simple Regression Model

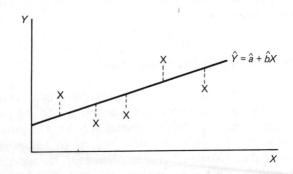

mised in regression analysis. A different equation would be produced if horizontal distances were minimised. Thus, it is important to distinguish clearly between the dependent and independent variables. The least squares regression model minimises differences between the observed and estimated values of the dependent variable.

Various statistical equations are available in order to determine the values of $\hat{a}$ and $\hat{b}$ in equation (4.4). The reader is referred to a standard econometrics textbook (such as Johnston, 1984) for the derivation of these equations. An example of simple regression using the so-called 'normal equations' is set out in Table 4.1. Various summations of the basic data, ΣX, ΣY, ΣX^2 and ΣXY, and the number of observations, n, are inserted into the equations and the values of $\hat{a}$ and $\hat{b}$ computed. In practice, however, these values will usually be computed using a computer package.

The underlying equation, i.e., equation (4.3), included an error term, e. The least squares regression model makes specific assumptions about the properties of this error term. It is important to recognise the nature of these properties, because if they are not met in a particular regression problem, the estimates of a and b will be affected. The following are the assumed properties:

(i) The mean of the error term is zero.
(ii) The values of the error terms e_i and e_j associated with any two values of X are independent.
(iii) There is a constant variance of the error term for all observed values of X.

The independence and constant variance properties of the error term require careful consideration, as they could be violated in a number of accounting contexts. For instance, if cost and output data are collected over a number of periods, cyclical or seasonal variations in the data could create consistent relationships in the error term. In such a case, the problem of autocorrelation, also known as serial-correlation, is said to exist.

A similar problem arises in the data illustrated in Figure 4.2. In that case six observations of costs and output were obtained. Taken at face value, a quite satisfactory regression line could be fitted to the data. But when it is recognised that the numbering of the observations corresponds to successive time periods, it can be

TABLE 4.1
Example of Simple Regression and Correlation

| BASIC DATA | | | | |
| Overhead cost per quarter £'000 | Units produced £'000 | | | |
Y	X	XY	X^2	Y^2
20	5	100	25	400
16	3	48	9	256
24	7	168	49	576
22	5	110	25	484
18	4	72	16	324
$\Sigma Y = 100$	$\Sigma X = 24$	$\Sigma XY = 498$	$\Sigma X^2 = 124$	$\Sigma Y^2 = 2040$

$n = 5$ (i.e., number of observations)

Normal equations
(1) $\Sigma Y = n\hat{a} + \hat{b}\Sigma X$ (1) $100 = 5\hat{a} + 24\hat{b}$
(2) $\Sigma XY = \hat{a}\Sigma X + \hat{b}\Sigma X^2$ (2) $498 = 24\hat{a} + 124\hat{b}$
from (1) $\hat{a} = 20 - 4.8\hat{b}$
Substituting into (2) $498 = 24(20 - 4.8\hat{b}) + 124\hat{b}$
             $18 = 8.8\hat{b}$
             $\hat{b} = 2.05$
And $\hat{a} = 20 - 4.8(2.05)$ $\hat{a} = 10.16$
Thus $\hat{Y} = 10.16 + 2.05X$

Correlation coefficient

$$r = \frac{n\Sigma XY - \Sigma X \Sigma Y}{\sqrt{n\Sigma X^2 - (\Sigma X)^2}\ \sqrt{n\Sigma X^2 - (\Sigma Y)^2}}$$

$$= \frac{5(498) - (24)(100)}{\sqrt{5(124) - (24)^2}\ \sqrt{5(2040) - (100)^2}} = \frac{90}{\sqrt{44}\ \sqrt{200}}$$

$$r = 0.96$$

FIGURE 4.2
An Illustration of Cost/Output Data

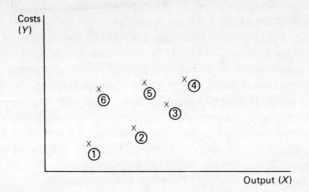

seen that when output was rising, costs were increasing at a particular rate. But when output subsequently declined (in periods 4–6), the costs declined at a much slower rate. These different rates of change may be due to the costs of shedding labour, disposing of capital equipment, and so on. If a simple regression line was fitted in such a case, the values of the error term would not be independent; each value would depend on the previous value.

If the constant variance property is violated, the problem of heteroscedasticity is said to exist. This is quite easy to envisage in an accounting problem. If costs and output are low, it is likely that there will be some range in which the actual costs will vary around the expected cost. For instance, at a low level of output with expected costs of £1 000, the range for costs may be plus or minus £200. However, if the costs associated with a much larger output are, say, £100 000, the range for costs is likely to be rather greater than plus or minus £200 – for instance it might be plus or minus £2 000 or even £20 000. In such a case it might be appropriate to think in terms of a constant proportion around the expected value – but this would violate the constant variance property of the error term.

4.3   Some Other Problems

(i) Regression analysis uses data obtained from past observations to estimate the relationship between the independent and dependent variables. It can sometimes be difficult to obtain sufficient data for a satisfactory estimate of the regression equation. Data is usually obtained by observing the relevant variables over a number of time periods. But, as will be discussed below, historical observations, particularly from periods in the distant past, can be of doubtful validity. In the case of a large company, however, it may be possible to increase the data available without going too far into the past by observing a number of similar operations; for example, different factories producing similar products. It is a general rule in regression analysis that 'the more data the better', but only if the data is comparable.

(ii) When using historical data from several time periods, it is important to identify shifts which may have occurred in the relationship between the dependent and independent variables. For instance, if cost is the dependent variable and output is the independent variable, any change in production methods could cause a structural shift in the regression equation. In such a case, only data which reflects the current structural relationship should be used – although it may be possible in some circumstances to suitably modify the earlier data. A similar problem can occur when cost data is affected by inflation. Unless the raw data is adjusted to reflect a constant price level, the relationship expressed in the regression equation could be distorted.

(iii) In almost all cases, regression analysis will generate an equation. Thus it is important to question whether the equation is satisfactory. In the following section some tests of the adequacy of a regression model will be discussed, but for the present it is sufficient to note that in some cases there may be an apparent relationship between a dependent and an independent variable, when no direct relationship actually exists. For instance, corresponding increases in expenditure on alcohol and cars may not imply a propensity for drunken driving, rather they may both reflect increases in an underlying variable, such as the gross national product – as output in the economy increases, the sales of both alcohol and motor-cars may also increase. Accordingly, a regression equation should only be used if there is a *prima facie* case for the relationship which is suggested by the model. If the model does not make intuitive sense, it should be treated with considerable caution.

4.4 Testing the Adequacy of the Model

Let us assume that it has been possible to obtain sufficient data and that the data has been processed by a computer regression package which has estimated a regression equation. It is now important to question the adequacy of our estimated equation. The following discussion examines three particular issues:

(i) The strength of the relationship between X and Y.
(ii) The adequacy of a linear model.
(iii) The validity of the assumptions made by regression analysis – especially those concerning the error term.

The strength of the relationship

The principal means of measuring the strength of the relationship between the dependent and independent variables is the correlation coefficient. This coefficient, r, measures the extent to which the dependent and independent variables co-vary. There are a number of formulae which can be used to compute the correlation coefficient, one of the more popular is as follows:

$$r = \frac{n\Sigma XY - \Sigma X \Sigma Y}{\sqrt{n\Sigma X^2 - (\Sigma X)^2} \ \sqrt{n\Sigma Y^2 - (\Sigma Y)^2}} \tag{4.6}$$

The meanings of the terms in the formula are illustrated by the example shown in Table 4.1. The value of the correlation coefficient will be in the range -1 to $+1$. A coefficient of $+1$ indicates that the dependent and independent variables are perfectly positively correlated, whereas a coefficient of -1 indicates that the two variables are perfectly negatively correlated. A correlation coefficient of zero, however, indicates that there is no linear relationship between the two variables. Accordingly, the greater the distance from zero, in either the positive or negative direction, the stronger the relationship between the two variables. In order to avoid the sign of the correlation coefficient when assessing the strength of the relationship between the dependent and independent variables, the value of r^2 is usually considered. In the case of multiple correlation, which will be considered later, an equivalent measure is used – the coefficient of multiple determination, R^2.

Adequacy of a linear model

If there is no linear relationship between the dependent and independent variables, the regression equation will look like the horizontal line shown in Figure 4.3. In that case, the regression equation takes the form $\hat{Y}=\hat{a}$, where $\hat{a}$ is the mean of the Y observations. In such a case, the value of $\hat{b}$ is zero and the regression has no explanatory power – for any value of X, the best estimate of Y is the mean of the observed values of Y. Two approaches are available to test the adequacy of the linear model:

(i) The hypothesis that the value of $\hat{b}$ in the regression equation is significantly different from zero can be tested.
(ii) The variation in the dependent variable which is explained by the model can be analysed – this is known as the analysis of variance.

FIGURE 4.3
Regression with No Linear Relationship

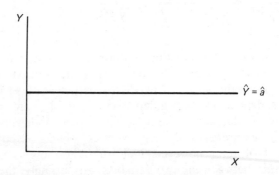

In simple regression these two approaches lead to similar conclusions, although they make use of different statistics. The former uses a t statistic, whereas the latter uses the F statistic. (In multiple regression, however, the F statistic will be easier to use, as there will be more than one independent variable to be considered.)

The t statistic is formed by dividing the estimate of b, i.e., $\hat{b}$, by its standard error. The significance of $\hat{b}$ can then be tested by comparing the size of this t statistic with the standard values for t given in statistical tables. However, a useful rule-of-thumb is that for a reasonable sample size (say, n greater than 30), $t \geq 2$ indicates that $\hat{b}$ is significantly different from zero at a 95 per cent level of confidence, and $t \geq 3$ indicates a significant $\hat{b}$ at 99.8 per cent level of confidence.

The r^2 (or R^2 in the case of multiple regression) measures the variation in Y, which is explained by the regression equation. The total variation in the observed values of Y will comprise two elements: (1) the variation explained by the estimated equation, and (2) the variation which remains in the error term. The F statistic is obtained by dividing the variance explained by the estimated equation, by the variance remaining in the error term. Thus, if the estimated equation explains all the variation in Y, the value of F will be infinite; as the F statistic will be formed by dividing 100 per cent by 0 per cent. At the other end of the range, the value of F will be zero when the estimated equation explains none of the variation in Y. Accordingly, when there is no linear relationship, the value of F will be zero.

In general, the strength of the linear relationship is indicated by the size of the F statistic – the higher the F statistic the stronger the linear relationship. As with the t statistic, there are tables which give critical limits for the F statistic. Once again, there are some convenient rules-of-thumb. For a reasonable sample size (say, n greater than 30), $F \geq 4$ indicates a significant linear relationship at a 95 per cent level of confidence, and $F \geq 8$ implies such a relationship at a 99 per cent level of confidence.

Validity of assumptions about the error term

If the assumptions concerning the error term described earlier are not valid, the estimated equation may prove unreliable. Three assumptions were mentioned: (1) a mean of zero, (2) independence, and (3) constant variance.

The least squares regression technique forces the mean of the estimated error terms (i.e., estimated from the observations) to equal zero. But this need not imply that the error term in the underlying equation has a mean of zero. This, in fact, is the most difficult of the three assumptions to verify. As a result it is often taken for granted. Nevertheless, some indications of its validity can be obtained from the pattern of the estimated error terms.

Plotting estimated error terms can provide a simple method for examining the assumptions of independence and constant variance, as well as for assessing the validity of the zero mean assumption. Estimated values of the error term can be determined by subtracting the value of $\hat{Y}$ (computed using the estimated equation) for each observed value of X, from the corresponding observation of Y. Such calculations can be expressed mathematically as follows.

$$\hat{e}_i = Y_i - \hat{Y}_i \tag{4.7}$$

A plot of the error terms against time and against the dependent or the independent variable may indicate whether autocorrelation or heteroscedasticity are present in the data, as will be explained below. In addition, runs of $\hat{e}_i$ with the same sign may suggest that the zero mean assumption could be invalid. For example, although the mean of $\hat{e}_i$ will be zero, a run of positive values followed by a run of negative values could cast doubt on the zero mean assumption.

Autocorrelation

Figure 4.4 indicates the possibility of autocorrelation, as there is a distinct pattern in the error term through time. Autocorrelation can arise because there is some systematic variation in the dependent variable which is not explained by the estimated equation and accordingly, it remains in the error term. One means of removing such systematic variation from the error term is to add additional independent variables to the model. These additional variables may capture the systematic variation which is currently in

FIGURE 4.4
A Simple Check for Autocorrelation

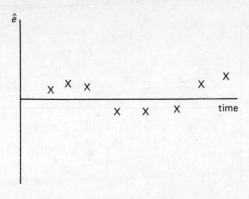

the error term, thereby giving an equation with only random variations in the error term. This approach requires an application of multiple regression which will be discussed later. An alternative means of removing autocorrelation from the error term is to revise the model by, for instance, using the change in the dependent variable and the change in the independent variable through time in place of the absolute values of those variables. Other estimating techniques (termed generalised least squares) may also be used and the reader is referred to econometrics textbooks on the subject for further information, for example Johnston (1984) and Maddala (1988).

Many computer packages give an indication of autocorrelation through a 'Durbin-Watson' statistic. This statistic can take values in the range zero to 4. Values in the region of 2 indicate no autocorrelation, while values tending towards zero or 4 indicate the possibility of autocorrelation.

Heteroscedasticity

This problem occurs when the variance of the error term is not constant. The plot of the error terms in Figure 4.5 indicates the

FIGURE 4.5
A Simple Check for Heteroscedasticity

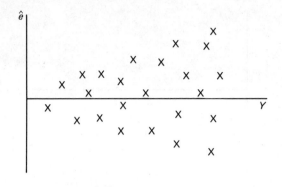

possibility of heteroscedasticity. In that case, the size of the error terms appear to increase with increases in the value of Y. Such a problem could exist when there is growth through time in the dependent variable, or when inflation increases the magnitude of the values on the dependent variable. Various revisions to the model could be tried in an attempt to remove heteroscedasticity. For example, a model of the form,

$$\frac{\hat{Y}}{t} = \hat{a} + \hat{b}X \qquad (4.8)$$

where t is a measure of time, could be used to eliminate the effects of growth through time. Alternatively, the dependent variable could be deflated by a price index.

4.5   Use of the Model

Once the model has been estimated and its adequacy tested to our satisfaction, we can then proceed to use the model. However, one further test might be considered: 'Does the resulting model make intuitive sense?' If, for instance, an equation relating costs to output indicates a negative value for $\hat{b}$, great care should be exercised before using the model. Such a value for $\hat{b}$ suggests that total costs decrease as output increases. Whilst there may be circumstances in which such a situation could arise, they will be highly unusual. Even if statistical tests have proved satisfactory, such a model should not be used, unless it appears that the rather unusual circumstances of declining total costs appear reasonable.

If regression analysis has been used to identify fixed and variable costs, the estimated equation will provide 'point' estimates for these two parameters. However, as with all statistics, point estimates are only one of a range of possible values. The range for the fixed and variable costs can be determined using the standard errors of $\hat{a}$ and $\hat{b}$. For instance, at a 95 per cent level of confidence, the value of $\hat{a}$ or $\hat{b}$ will lie within two standard errors of the estimated value. For 99.8 per cent confidence, plus or minus three standard errors could be used. Most computer packages will provide the values of the standard errors of $\hat{a}$ and $\hat{b}$.

If regression analysis has been used to predict some future value(s) of the dependent variable, given some predicted value(s) for the independent variable, then the estimated equation can be used to determine the estimate(s) for $\hat{Y}$. Once again such an estimate is the mid-point of a range which can be expressed in terms of the standard error of the estimated $\hat{Y}$ (or equivalently the standard deviation of the error term). But, when determining the range for a particular forecast of Y, certain adjustments to the standard error are needed before use can be made of the rule-of-thumb of two or three standard errors for 95 per cnt or 99.8 per cent levels of confidence. The formula in equation (4.9) computes the standard error of the forecast, S_f, by modifying the standard error of $\hat{Y}$, S_e, to reflect the sample size, and the distance of the forecast value from the mean of the observations used to determine the estimated equation:

$$S_f = S_e \sqrt{1 + \frac{1}{n} + \frac{(X_f - \overline{X})^2}{\Sigma(X_i - \overline{X})^2}}$$

(4.9)

In this expression, the term X_f is the value of the independent variable for which a forecast of the dependent variable is required. If this value is a considerable distance from the mean of the values which were used to estimate the regression equation, then the then the resulting forecast is likely to be more uncertain than if it were closer to the mean. The third term within the square root in equation (4.9) makes an appropriate adjustment. The further the forecast, X_f, is from the mean of the values used in the regression, $\overline{X}$, the greater the standard error of the forecast, S_f.

The second term in the square root in equation (4.9), $1/n$, adjusts the standard error of the forecast for sample size. The smaller the number of observations, n, used for the regression, the larger the term $1/n$ and, accordingly, the larger the standard error of the forecast.

Once the standard error of the forecast is calculated, the range for the forecast of Y can be computed by taking two (or three) standard errors of the forecast, S_f, around the 'point estimate' of $\hat{Y}$, for a 95 per cent (or 99.8 per cent) level of confidence.

It is worth noting at this point that the above discussion indicates the way in which statistical analysis forces a recognition of uncertainty. Although the nature of the underlying distributions may be known, estimates derived from these distributions are uncertain. For example, ranges of possible values for total costs, forecast sales, etc., are obtained, rather than single (certain) values. Thus, the use of statistical methods represents a movement away from the certainty models of management accounting's conventional wisdom. To make full use of statistical analysis for cost estimation and forecasting, however, it is necessary to go beyond the simple regression model and to consider multiple regression.

4.6 Multiple Regression

As indicated earlier in this chapter, multiple regression is used to estimate a model which has one dependent variable, together with two or more independent variables. For instance, consider a business which produces three products. A model relating total costs and the production of each of the three products could be expressed as follows:

$$Y = a + b_1X_1 + b_2X_2 + b_3X_3 + e \tag{4.10}$$

where Y is total costs, a is the total fixed cost and b_1, b_2, b_3 are the variable costs for each of the three products.

The principles and issues discussed earlier in connection with simple regression also apply to multiple regression. But there are some additional problems associated with multiple regression; in particular, the problem of multicollinearity which will be discussed later. Multiple regression, however, offers possibilities for overcoming some of the other problems of regression analysis. In discussing autocorrelation earlier in this chapter, it was suggested that additional variables could be added to a model, to capture some of the systematic variation remaining in the error term. Variables such as weight of products produced, direct labour hours used, and so on could be added to a regression equation. Furthermore, multiple regression offers the possibility of using artificial variables, usually known as dummy variables. Their nature and use are described below.

Dummy variables

These variables usually take only a limited number of values; for instance, either zero or 1. They are particularly useful for capturing characteristics of the world which can be expressed only in discrete terms. As an illustration, consider the observations plotted on Figure 4.6. Simple regression could be used to fit the

FIGURE 4.6
Regression of Total Costs on Output

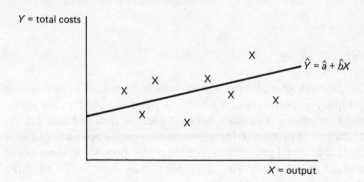

line indicated. However, if autocorrelation is found, and it is noticed that the values of Y which lie above the estimated line are associated with costs in the winter months and the observations of Y lying below the estimated line are costs in the summer months, it may be concluded that there is a seasonal variation in cost patterns. A revised model of the form:

$$\hat{Y} = \hat{a} + \hat{b}_1 X + \hat{b}_2 S \qquad (4.11)$$

could be estimated using multiple regression. The dummy variable, S, takes a value of zero if the observation is in a summer month and a value of 1 if in a winter month. The estimated equation would now capture the additional fixed costs associated with operating in the winter (for example, the additional heating and lighting costs). The costs at different times of the year could then be expressed as follows:

$$\text{Summer } \hat{Y} = \hat{a} + \hat{b}_1 X$$
$$\text{Winter } \hat{Y} = (\hat{a} + \hat{b}_2) + \hat{b}_1 X \qquad (4.12)$$

In summer months, the variable S takes a value of zero and so the parameters $\hat{a}$ and $\hat{b}_1$ indicate the fixed and variable costs of production, whereas in winter months the variable S takes a value of 1 giving an additional constant term, $\hat{b}_2$, which is added to the fixed costs. Such a procedure can remove the autocorrelation associated with seasonal variation in fixed costs. Techniques are also available for adding a dummy variable to the b parameter – this would handle seasonal variation in the variable costs. Other possibilities for removing alternative sources of autocorrelation are also available through the use of dummy variables.

Multicollinearity

The problem of multicollinearity, which exists only in the case of multiple regression, occurs when independent variables are themselves correlated. Consider, for example, the data in Table 4.2. As the output of product P increases, the output of products Q and R increase in direct proportion. Although it is possible to identify the increase in costs following a proportionate increase in all three products, it is impossible to identify the separate effect on costs of increasing the production of any one of the products. In this case of perfect correlation between the three products, the parameters of the regression equation could not be estimated. However, only the smallest deviation from these perfect proportions would be required to make the estimation of a regression equation possible. But in such a case the variation in costs due to a minimal change in the output of the individual products would be insufficient for reliable estimates of the variable costs of each product. Although an equation relating products *P, Q* and *R* to total costs could provide a reasonable forecast of costs, provided the product mix remains unchanged, the individual estimates of the variable costs for the three products would be extremely unreliable as they would involve extrapolations from very small changes.

TABLE 4.2
An Illustration of Multicollinearity

	Product (units)		Total
P	*Q*	*R*	Costs (£)
50	20	10	1 650
60	24	12	1 800
70	28	14	1 950
80	32	16	2 100
90	36	18	2 250

Multicollinearity exists whenever there are substantial correlations between two or more independent variables in a regression equation. The problem could be avoided either by working only in terms of the aggregate product, for instance, a batch of products *P, Q* and *R* in the standard mix, or by using some other unit of production, for example machine hours. A regression model relating total costs to machine hours would yield an estimate of the variable costs per machine hour which could be used to determine the costs of producing individual products, given their individual machine hour requirements.

Illustration

Table 4.3 gives some illustrative data comprising overhead costs for the last twelve months, together with various indices of activity. This data will be used to estimate an equation relating overhead costs to the level of activity. A number of possibilities will be examined using various combinations of the four available measures of activity: units produced, direct labour hours, machine hours, and weight of units produced. A computer package has been used to estimate a variety of regression equations – the estimated equations and related statistics are set out in Table 4.4. In order to select the 'best' equation we will look initially at the R^2 and F statistics which indicate the strength of the relationship and the adequacy of the linear model. We will also look at the standard error of $\hat{Y}$ as this will directly affect the confidence interval of any forecasts made with the equation. The discussion earlier in this chapter indicated that we should be looking for high values of R^2 and F, together with a low standard error of $\hat{Y}$.

TABLE 4.3
Illustration: Data for Multiple Regression

Overhead costs per month	Units produced	Direct labour hours	Machine hours	Weight of units produced
£ 12 500	1 000	4 090	750	15 000
18 000	1 075	3 700	1 725	23 000
16 000	1 130	3 750	875	21 800
19 200	1 060	5 350	2 050	20 050
11 800	1 050	1 600	1 660	12 000
14 900	1 080	3 100	1 720	17 000
17 600	1 010	3 320	1 950	16 000
13 800	1 080	2 490	1 550	19 300
15 400	1 020	2 980	1 100	13 900
14 200	1 050	2 500	1 240	21 400
13 000	1 010	4 100	960	13 250
16 500	1 060	4 150	1 470	14 100

TABLE 4.4
Illustration: Estimated Equations and Selected Statistics

Model no.	X_1	X_2	X_3	X_4	Estimated equations*	DW	Fstat	R^2 (adj R^2)
1 Units					$Y = -2050 + 16.43(x_1)$ (2334.1) (−0.104) (0.878)	2.956	0.772	0.071 (−0.021)
2 DLH					$Y = 10562 + 1.36(x_1)$ (1969.2) (4.932) (2.265)	2.199	5.134	0.339 (0.273)
3 M/CH					$Y = 10955 + 3.016(x_1)$ (2005.5) (5.262) (2.143)	1.997	4.592	0.314 (0.246)
4 WT					$Y = 9777 + 0.317(x_1)$ (2077.6) (3.322) (1.896)	2.780	3.596	0.264 (0.190)
5 DLH M/CH					$Y = 6269 + 1.366(x_1) + 3.019(x_2)$ (1500.9) (2.829) (2.975) (2.866)	1.944	8.527	0.654 (0.577)
6 DLH M/CH WT					$Y = 3598 + 1.220(x_1) + 2.729(x_2) + 0.207(x_3)$ (1322.6) (1.493) (2.962) (2.901) (1.894)	2.645	8.516	0.761 (0.672)
7 DLH M/CH Units					$Y = -8249 + 1.393(x_1) + 2.854(x_2) + 0.139(x_3)$ (1471.1) (−0.654) (3.092) (2.739) (1.169)	2.226	6.372	0.704 (0.594)
8 DLH M/CH WT Units					$Y = 2283 + 1.229(x_1) + 2.726(x_2) + 0.198(x_3) + 0.137(x_4)$ (1413.1) (0.156) (2.724) (2.710) (1.292) (0.091)	2.656	5.597	0.762 (0.625)

* The term in parentheses on the left-hand side of each equation is the standard error of $\hat{Y}$ and the terms in parentheses on the right-hand side of each equation are the t statistics for the parameters immediately above.

The first four models shown in Table 4.4 are simple regressions using each of the four possible measures of activity in turn. The values for R^2 (or r^2 for these simple regressions) are highest for models 2 and 3. Thus, the next step is to look at model 5, i.e., the model containing the two measures of activity, direct labour hours and machine hours, which were the independent variables in models 2 and 3. The R^2 of 0.654 for this composite model is a substantial improvement over both of the simple models.

Whenever additional variables are added to a model, however, the R^2 will increase. This is because the new variable(s) will add to the explanatory power of the model. Unfortunately, each additional variable reduces the degrees of freedom which are available for estimating the parameters of the model. An adjusted R^2 can be computed to allow for the loss of degrees of freedom. This additional statistic is also shown in Table 4.4 – beneath the value for R^2. In terms of this statistic, model 5 still represents an improvement over models 2 and 3. Furthermore, model 5 is also superior to models 2 and 3 on the basis of both the F statistic and the standard error of $\hat{Y}$.

The next question to consider is whether the introduction of either the weight produced or the number of units produced would improve the model. Models 6 and 7 include these additional variables. Both model 6 and model 7 have a higher R^2 than model 5 and in both cases the adjusted R^2 has also increased, but by a quite small amount in the case of model 7. Although both models 6 and 7 have a lower F statistic than model 5, the reduction in the case of model 6 is quite small. The F statistic for both models 5 and 6 are significant at the 99 per cent level of confidence. Thus, models 5 and 6 appear superior to model 7. However, the choice between models 5 and 6 requires further consideration. As model 6 has a lower standard error of $\hat{Y}$ than model 5, it might appear that model 6 should be preferred. But we will leave this issue aside for the moment.

For the sake of completeness it would seem essential to examine a model with all four indices of activity, i.e., model 8. In comparison to model 6, model 8 has a lower adjusted R^2, a lower F statistic and a higher standard error of $\hat{Y}$. Model 8 also has a lower F statistic than model 5, although the former's adjusted R^2 is higher. On balance, however, model 8 does not seem to be an improvement over either model 5 or model 6.

Before going further, we should consider the interpretation of models 5 and 6. In the case of model 6 the variable costs all have positive signs and there is a positive fixed cost – this seems quite reasonable. However, although the t statistics on direct labour hours and machine hours are close to 3, which suggests a linear relationship (or equivalently, a parameter which is significantly different from zero) at a 99.8 per cent level of confidence, the t statistics on the constant term and on the weight of units produced are somewhat lower. The t statistics on the variables and constant term in model 5, however, look much more satisfactory. In fact, when we look generally at all four multiple regression models (i.e., models 5, 6, 7 and 8) only direct labour hours and machine hours have consistently significant t statistics. Thus, although both models 5 and 6 appear to be intuitively quite acceptable, the t statistics give particular support to model 5. Furthermore, the Durbin-Watson statistic for model 5 is very close to 2 (which indicates no autocorrelation) whereas for model 6 this statistic is some distance from 2. A Durbin-Watson statistic of 2.645 suggests a possibility of autocorrelation, but provides no clear evidence and should not give rise to undue concern.

The choice between models 5 and 6 is actually quite difficult. The individual parameters of model 5 appear to be more reliable; but as a total equation, model 6 looks quite attractive. Possibly the most appropriate conclusion is that model 6 is the better of the two if the regression equation is needed for forecasting overhead costs (specifically, because it has the lower standard error of $\hat{Y}$); whereas model 5 could be the better if estimates of fixed and variable costs are needed for decision making. Whichever model is preferred, it is important to test whether it satisfies the assumptions of regression analysis and, if not, an alternative model should be considered. To complete this illustration, it will be assumed that model 6 is preferred and subjected to further testing.

Table 4.5 sets out the correlation coefficients between each pair of independent variables in model 6. In each case, the r^2 is very close to zero. Thus, there is no evidence of multicollinearity. Table 4.6 uses the selected equation to estimate the error terms. These error terms sum to zero, as they always do with the ordinary least squares technique. As can be seen in Figure 4.7, there are no clear patterns which might cause us to question the assumptions concerning the error term. However, although the plot of the error terms against time does not indicate a consistent pattern, there is a hint of symmetry about the horizontal axis. This could explain the Durbin-Watson statistic of 2.645. But as mentioned above, there is no clear evidence of autocorrelation. Thus, model 6 seems reasonable. We can now go ahead and use the model to forecast overhead costs for future months, as described earlier.

TABLE 4.5
Illustration: Tests for Multicollinearity

Y	X	r	r^2 (adj r^2)
WT	DLH	0.184	0.034 (−0.062)
WT	M/CH	0.159	0.025 (−0.072)
M/CH	DLH	0.001	0.000 (−0.099)

4.7   Some Concluding Remarks

Statistical regression analysis is potentially a useful tool for management accounting, especially in planning and budgeting procedures. For instance, the demand for particular products, the availability of raw materials and the amount of overhead expenses could all be estimated using regression models. In addition, regression analysis can be used to separate costs into fixed and variable elements. For example, consider a steam generating plant which produces steam for two separate production processes. A regression model with one fixed, and two variable elements (one for each production process) could be used to estimate the variable cost for the steam required by each process. Many other similar opportunities exist for using regression analysis.

TABLE 4.6
Illustration: the Error Terms

Model 6 — the selected equation

$$\hat{Y} = 3598 + 1.220(DLH) + 2.729(M/CH) + 0.207(WT)$$

Overhead cost per month (Y_i)	$\hat{Y}_i$	$\hat{e}_i = Y_i - \hat{Y}_i$
£12 500	£13 754	£−1 254
18 000	17 604	396
16 000	15 095	905
19 200	19 891	−691
11 800	12 576	−776
14 900	15 610	−710
17 600	16 298	1 302
13 800	14 880	−1 080
15 400	13 127	2 273
14 200	14 483	−283
13 000	13 976	−976
16 500	15 606	894
		$\sum_i \hat{e}_i = 0$

The use of regression analysis for both cost estimation and forecasting could be deemed part of management accounting's conventional wisdom, as the techniques were widely discussed in the academic literature in the 1960s. However, as was indicated earlier, the use of statistical methods admits the possibility that uncertain estimates may be used in decision models. As such, regression analysis represents a step away from the certainty models which are associated with management accounting's conventional wisdom. In subsequent chapters we will see how the explicit recognition of uncertainty influenced the development of the management accounting literature.

FIGURE 4.7
Illustration: Plots of Error Term

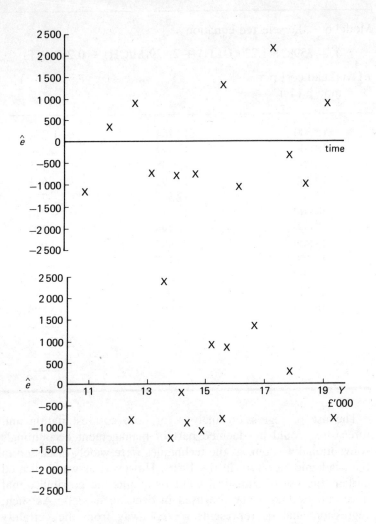

Cost–Volume–
Profit Analysis

5

The conditional truth approach of management accounting research in the 1960s which, as suggested earlier, underlies much of management accounting's conventional wisdom, relies on the specification of a decision model. At the end of Chapter 2 it was concluded that economics played a central role in structuring the decision models used by management accounting researchers in that decade. The decision maker was assumed to have available, at no cost and with no uncertainty, all the information needed to completely structure the decision problem and to achieve a profit maximising solution through an application of the principles of marginal analysis.

The first major change in the economic framework came about when researchers began to introduce uncertainty into their models. As already pointed out, the use of regression analysis for cost estimation encouraged, at least implicitly, the recognition that cost information is uncertain. By the end of the 1960s some writers had started to explore the implications of uncertainty. The early 1970s brought some major developments in this respect. This chapter explores the effects of introducing uncertainty into the analysis of cost–volume–profit (C–V–P) decisions. But first, however, it will be useful to describe the nature of C–V–P analysis, under conditions of certainty.

5.1 The Simple Model

The conventional C–V–P model assumes the existence of a single product which can be sold for a fixed price, p, that is independent of the quantity sold. The costs of producing this product comprise two elements: first, a fixed cost, a, which is independent of the quantity produced; and second, a unit variable cost, b, which will be incurred for each and every unit produced. These fixed and variable costs are assumed to be known with certainty and together to account for the total costs involved in producing the product. If the quantity sold is represented by x, then the following cost and revenue equations can be specified:

Total cost: $\qquad TC(x) = a + bx$ $\qquad\qquad$ (5.1)

Total revenue: $\quad TR(x) = px$ $\qquad\qquad$ (5.2)

These two equations can be combined to produce a profit function as follows:

Profit: $\qquad\qquad \pi(x) \;= px - (a + bx)$
$$= (p - b)x - a \qquad\qquad (5.3)$$

The term in brackets on the second line of expression (5.3), $(p - b)$, represents the unit contribution, selling price minus variable cost per unit, which will be earned on sales of this product. Thus, the profit equation can be expressed as the total contribution earned from sales quantity x, less the total fixed cost. Obviously, to break even the profit earned must equal zero.

The simple model set out in the above equations can be portrayed in the form of a cost–volume–profit chart as illustrated in Figure 5.1. This chart plots the profit earned for the various levels of output. The break-even point occurs where the profit equals zero. Such a simple chart can have value in disclosing the quantity of output which is needed in order to make production viable. This can be particularly important in a period of reduced economic activity. In addition to indicating break-even points, such charts can indicate the level of profit to be earned at various levels of output. Other uses of C–V–P charts include exploring the effects of changes in any of the variables, i.e., the selling price, the fixed cost and the variable cost.

FIGURE 5.1
Cost-Volume-Profit Chart

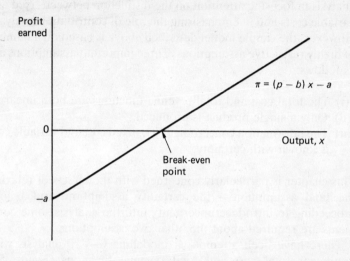

Probably the greatest attraction of C–V–P analysis is that it clearly demonstrates the importance of the contribution approach. The relationship between profit and contribution can be seen clearly in the profit function described above and illustrated in Figure 5.1. The break-even quantity can be defined in terms of contribution, by setting the profit equation (5.3) equal to zero and rearranging as follows:

$$\text{Break-even quantity: } x_{\text{BE}} = \frac{a}{p - b} \tag{5.4}$$

In other words, the break-even quantity can be found by dividing the fixed cost by the contribution per unit. A simple extension of this approach can be used to determine the quantity needed to produce any required level of profit. Most textbooks will contain numerous illustrations of the way in which contribution can be used within a C–V–P framework to analyse output decisions.

5.2   Assumptions

The foregoing discussion highlights the usefulness of C–V–P analysis in focusing attention on the distinction between fixed and variable costs and in emphasising the role of contribution analysis. However, the simple model described above is based on a number of highly restrictive assumptions. Three important assumptions are as follows:

   (i) The total cost and total revenue functions are both linear.
  (ii) Only a single product is produced.
 (iii) The information concerning price, fixed cost and variable cost is known with certainty.

This chapter is particularly concerned with the effects of relaxing the final assumption – the certainty assumption. But before proceeding to introduce uncertainty into the analysis some comments are required about the other two assumptions.

There have been attempts at modelling C–V–P analysis with non-linear total cost and total revenue functions. Figure 5.2 illustrates the possible form of a non-linear model, which is consistent with standard economic theory. The functions illustrated give rise to two separate break-even points and also indicate the maximum profit which can be earned. While it may be possible to draw a graph of such functions, it is extremely difficult to determine the corresponding mathematical expressions. Accordingly, the accounting literature has not pursued such an approach. It is frequently argued that within the relevant range (i.e., the range within which any production decision would fall) the sections of the non-linear functions can be approximated by straight lines.

The extension of the simple C–V–P model to accommodate multiple products is relatively easy if there is a standard product mix – in other words, if the products are sold in fixed proportions. Where there is no standard product mix, there will be no unique break-even point. However, if constraints, for instance, in the form of limited productive resources are added to the production mix problem, a unique solution may be obtained, but expressed in terms of the maximum profits rather than a break-even point. The solutions to such problems are usually derived through the use of

FIGURE 5.2
Non-Linear Cost and Revenue Functions

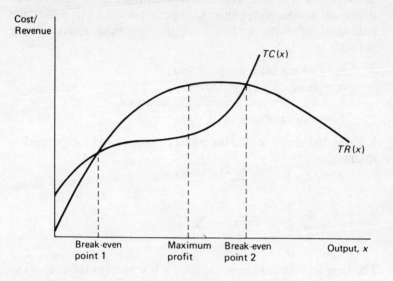

mathematical programming techniques, particularly linear programming – as we discussed in Chapter 2.

The difficulties experienced by researchers who have attempted to integrate uncertainty into linear programming models has led to an emphasis on sensitivity analysis. This has meant that uncertainty is normally dealt with outside the decision model. Linear programming is used to generate solutions based on various assumptions about the future and to indicate the range of applicability of each solution. The decision maker is then expected to evaluate subjectively the uncertainty surrounding each set of assumptions. This approach contrasts with the attempts of other researchers to integrate uncertainty directly into C–V–P analysis. Before exploring the implications of the work of these researchers, the nature of C–V–P analysis in a multiproduct situation, with certainty and a standard product mix, will be described. This will provide the basis for a subsequent discussion of extensions for uncertainty in multiproduct C–V–P analysis.

5.3   Multiproduct C–V–P Analysis

In order to extend the simple C–V–P model to handle the situation in which a firm produces more than one product, it is necessary to define the products carefully. Using the subscript i to denote the individual products, $i=1, \ldots, n$, the following terms can be defined:

p_i = selling price for product i,
a_i = fixed cost for product i,
b_i = variable cost per unit for product i,
x_i = output of product i.

Using the above terms, the profit equation can be expressed as follows:

$$\pi = \sum_i p_i x_i - \sum_i (a_i + b_i x_i)$$

$$= \sum_i (p_i - b_i) x_i - \sum_i a_i \qquad (5.5)$$

The final term in the above expression is written as the sum of the fixed costs on each of the n products. However, it may only be possible to identify the total fixed costs for the organisation as a whole – in this case the final term could be represented by a constant term, say, A.

If it is assumed that there are three products, X, Y and Z, then the C–V–P chart illustrated in Figure 5.3 could be drawn. This chart was constructed for a total output of V, using an assumed standard product mix for the three products. The total fixed costs of A are not traceable to individual products. At an output of zero the profit earned will amount to $-A$ (i.e., a loss of A), represented by point k on the chart. The line km represents the profit earned by product X – the slope of the line is determined by the contribution per unit earned on sales of that product. The line mn represents the profit earned by product Y, which has a lesser contribution per unit than product X. The line nj is the profit earned by the least profitable product, i.e., product Z. A line which joins the points k and j reflects the average profitability of the three products and each point on that line represents the profit earned for the associated output, assuming that the three products

FIGURE 5.3
Multiproduct C-V-P Chart

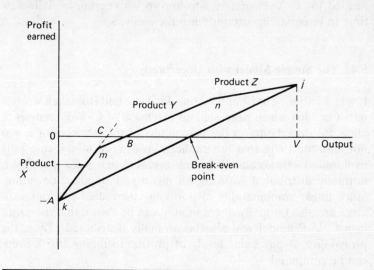

are sold in the standard product mix, i.e., the mix implied in the construction of the chart. Accordingly, the indicated break-even point only applies if the products are sold in that standard product mix. It can be seen clearly from Figure 5.3 that break-even can occur at lower levels of output provided that proportions of the products are changed. For instance, the point, *B*, where the line *kmnj* crosses the horizontal axis indicates a possible break-even point.

The line *kmnj* reflects the amounts of the three products included in a total output of *V*, using the standard product mix. Break-even at *B* could be achieved by producing the quantity of product X implied in the total production of *V*, together with a small amount of product Y. But the necessary combination of X and Y is not a standard product mix. Break-even could also be achieved at point *C*, provided that only the most profitable product, X, is produced. Thus, as indicated earlier, if the assumption of a standard product mix is relaxed, there will be no unique break-even point. But with a standard product mix a unique break-even point can be determined using C–V–P analysis, as is illustrated in Figure 5.3.

So far it has been assumed that the selling price and cost data needed for C–V–P analysis are known with certainty. It is now time to integrate uncertainty into the analysis.

5.4   The Simple Model with Uncertainty

It was mentioned in Chapter 2 that Jaedicke and Robichek wrote a paper in 1964 which suggested an extension of C–V–P analysis to allow for uncertainty in the parameters of the model. But it was not until the 1970s that the implications of uncertainty were fully explored. Jaedicke and Robichek assumed that sales quantity is normally distributed with known mean and standard deviation. Since linear combinations of normally distributed random variables are also normally distributed, it can be shown that the profit in a C–V–P model will also be normally distributed. Thus, the probability of particular levels of profits, including break-even, can be computed.

In the simple model of a single product firm described earlier in this chapter, all the variables were assumed to be known with certainty. In principle, any of the variables could be subject to uncertainty. However, Jaedicke and Robichek only considered uncertainty concerning the quantity which can be sold. It will be assumed that this quantity is a random variable, $\tilde{x}$ (a tilde will be used to indicate a random variable), which is normally distributed with a mean of μ and a standard deviation of σ_x. This normally distributed random variable can be written mathematically as follows:

$$\tilde{x} \sim N(\mu, \sigma_x) \tag{5.6}$$

Now using the simple profit function,

$$\pi(x) = (p - b)x - a \tag{5.7}$$

it follows that profit will also be a normally distributed variable, expressed in the following terms:

$$\tilde{\pi} \sim N((p-b)\mu - a, (p-b)\sigma_x) \tag{5.8}$$
$$\text{or} \quad \tilde{\pi} \sim N(E\tilde{\pi}), (p-b)\sigma_x) \tag{5.8}$$

where $E(\tilde{\pi}) = (p-b)\mu - a$.

In words, profit will be normally distributed with a mean equal to the expected value of the profits and with a standard deviation equal to the unit contribution multiplied by the standard deviation of the quantity sold. Once such values are determined it is a relatively easy task to compute the probability of breaking even. Consider the following illustration.

A company producing a single product regards its sales volume as normally distributed with a mean of 10 500 units, and a standard deviation of 2 000 units. Formally, this can be expressed as:

$$\bar{x} \sim N(10\,500, 2\,000) \tag{5.9}$$

If the selling price, p, is £10 and the variable cost, b, is £8, with fixed costs, a, of £20 000, then the profit distribution can be calculated as follows:

$$\begin{aligned}
E(\bar{\pi}) &= (10-8)\,\mu - 20\,000 \\
&= (10-8)\,10\,500 - 20\,000 = 1\,000 \\
\sigma_\pi &= (10-8)\sigma_x \\
&= (10-8)\,2\,000 = 4\,000
\end{aligned}$$

Thus, $\bar{\pi} \sim N(1\,000, 4\,000)$ \hfill (5.10)

In words, profit is normally distributed, with a mean of £1 000 and a standard deviation of £4 000.

Using the relationship between fixed costs and contribution per unit derived earlier, see equation (5.4), the break-even point can be calculated as follows:

$$x_{BE} = \frac{a}{p-b}$$

$$= \frac{20\,000}{2} = 10\,000 \text{ units} \tag{5.11}$$

This calculation indicates that an output of 10 000 units is required to break even. The mean of the sales distribution is a little higher at 10 500 units. So what is the probability of breaking even in this case?

Figure 5.4 illustrates the profit distribution in the form of a normal distribution with a mean of £1 000 and a standard deviation of £4 000. The probability of breaking even is given by the area under the curve which falls to the right of the dotted vertical line

FIGURE 5.4
Profit Distribution

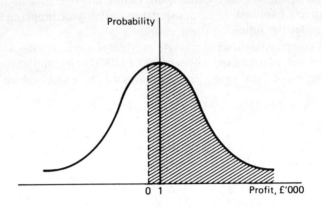

placed at the level of zero profits. From knowledge of the normal
distribution, it is known that 50 per cent of the area under the
curve falls to the right of the mean. In order to calculate the
probability of breaking even, the area under the curve between the
break-even point and the mean of the distribution is also needed.
This distance can be expressed in terms of standard deviations.
The break-even point is $1\,000/4\,000$ standard deviations from the
mean (i.e., $0.25\sigma_\pi$). A table of areas under the normal curve
(which can be found in most statistics books) discloses that 0.25
standard deviations represents approximately 10 per cent of the
area under the curve. Thus the probability of at least breaking
even, or in other words, of achieving a profit in excess of zero, is
60 per cent, i.e., the 10 per cent probability of profits being
between zero and £1 000, and the 50 per cent probability of profits
being £1 000 or more.

5.5 Limitations

The analysis described above is likely to encounter a number of
problems when attempts are made to apply it in practice. These

difficulties arise from both the simplicity and the complexity of the analysis. This apparently contradictory statement refers, on the one hand, to the complexities of the data required for the above analysis and, on the other, to the simplicity of the model which ignores many of the potentially relevant characteristics of problems found in practice; in particular, the model described above deals with uncertainty in only one variable.

In practice it is likely to be very difficult to obtain realistic estimates of the mean and standard deviation of the sales distribution and, as a result, the reliability of the derived profit distributions will be questionable.

The parameters on the sales distribution could be obtained either by reference to historic data or by eliciting the subjective estimates of managers. Historic data has the attraction of appearing objective, but frequently there may not be sufficient observations for reliable estimates. Furthermore, as observations are likely to be related over time, problems of autocorrelation may lead to biased estimates of the standard deviation.

The absence of acceptable historic data has led to suggestions that attempts should be made to elicit subjective estimates from managers. The techniques used for this purpose usually involve asking managers to compare the likelihood of particular sales volumes with certain hypothetical gambles. Such techniques, however, have been dismissed as impracticable by a number of writers.

The analysis outlined above relied on the assumption that uncertainty concerning the sales volume can be described by a normal distribution. This assumption is not essential however, provided there is no uncertainty in any of the other variables. If historic or subjective estimates can be made of the probabilities of particular levels of output it may be possible to fit a polynomial to the data in order to derive a cumulative probability function, which expresses the probabilities of achieving *at least* particular volumes of sales. The function can then be used to determine probabilities of breaking even. This approach has not been particularly popular in the literature because it cannot be extended to situations where uncertainty exists in other variables. But, in such situations, even the assumptions of normal distributions are not altogether satisfactory, as will be discussed later.

A further limitation of the above analysis relates to its single product character. However, it is relatively simple to extend the analysis to deal with multiple products, provided that the normal distribution assumptions can be retained. In this case, the sales volume for the various products will be assumed to have a joint multivariate normal distribution.

5.6 Multiproduct C–V–P Analysis Under Uncertainty

In addition to defining a mean and standard deviation of the sales distributions for each of the products, it is now necessary to consider the correlations between each pair of products. The distribution of each product's sales can be expressed in the terms used in previous sections as follows:

$$\tilde{x}_i \sim N(\mu_i, \sigma_i) \tag{5.12}$$

In addition, the covariance between the sales of each pair of products can be defined as

$$\text{cov}(\tilde{x}_i, \tilde{x}_j) \equiv \sigma_{ij} \tag{5.13}$$

where

$\sigma_{ii} = \sigma_i^2$ (the variance of sales of product i)
$\sigma_{ij} = \sigma_i \sigma_j \rho_{ij}$
$\rho_{ij} =$ the correlation coefficient between the sales of product i and product j

Now if p_i, b_i and a_i represent the selling price, variable cost and fixed cost of the ith product, the profit function can be expressed as follows:

$$\tilde{\pi} = \sum_i (p_i - b_i)\tilde{x}_i - \sum_i a_i \tag{5.14}$$

As indicated above, the sales for the $x_1, \dots, x_n$ products are assumed to have a joint multivariate normal distribution. As any linear combination of such random variables will also be normally distributed, the profit function will have a univariate normal distribution with the following parameters:

$$E(\tilde{\pi}) = \sum_i (p_i - b_i)\mu_i - \sum_i a_i \tag{5.15}$$

and

$$\text{Var}\,(\bar{\pi}) = E(\bar{\pi}^2) - (E\bar{\pi})^2$$

$$= \sum_i \sum_j (p_i - b_i)\sigma_{ij}(p_j - b_j)$$

$$= \sum_i (p_i - b_i)^2\,\sigma_i^2 + 2\sum_{i \neq j}\sum(p_i-b_i)(p_j-b_j)\sigma_i\sigma_j\sigma_{ij}$$

The expected profit expression is comparable with the single product case described earlier, but the variance of the profit distribution, $\text{Var}(\bar{\pi})$, is rather more complex. The best way to understand this expression is to use an illustration. (Any reader who wishes to see the derivation of this variance formula should consult a statistics textbook, such as Mood, Graybill and Boes, 1974, or a textbook on portfolio theory such as Dobbins and Witt, 1983.)

Consider a firm which sells two product lines both of which have expected sales of £5 000, a contribution of £1.25 and fixed costs of £5 800. But the standard deviation of the sales of product 1 is £200, whereas the standard deviation of the sales of product 2 is £400. The correlation between the two products, ρ_{12}, is 0.7. These figures have been adapted from an illustration devised by Johnson and Simik (1971).

The expected profit from sales of the two products can be calculated as follows:

$$
\begin{aligned}
E(\bar{\pi}) &= (p_1-b_1)\mu_1 - a_1 + (p_2-b_2)\mu_2 - a_2 \qquad (5.16)\\
&= 1.25(5\,000) - 5\,800 + 1.25(5\,000) - 5\,800\\
&= \quad\;\; 450 \quad + \quad\;\; 450 \quad = 900
\end{aligned}
$$

and the variance is:

$$
\begin{aligned}
\text{Var}\,(\bar{\pi}) &= (p_1-b_1)^2\,\sigma_1^2 + (p_2-b_2)^2\,\sigma_2^2\\
&\quad + 2(p_1-b_1)(p_2-b_2)\,\sigma_1\sigma_2\rho_{12} \qquad (5.17)\\
&= (1.25)^2\,(200)^2 + (1.25)^2\,(400)^2\\
&\quad + 2(1.25)(1.25)(200)(400)0.7\\
&= 62\,500 + 250\,000 + 175\,000\\
&= 487\,500
\end{aligned}
$$

And, $\quad \sigma_\pi = 698.2$

Thus, the parameters of the profit distribution which is assumed to be normal are known, i.e., $\bar{\pi} \sim N(900, 698.2)$. These parameters can be used to compute the probability of breaking even in exactly the same way as was described above in the case of a single product firm. But it is to be emphasised that a break-even point which is computed on the basis of expected sales volumes relies on the assumption of a standard product mix, as in the case of multiproduct C–V–P analysis under conditions of certainty described earlier in the chapter. Nevertheless, so long as these assumptions remain valid C–V–P analysis can be extended to conditions of uncertainty.

5.7   Uncertainty in Other Variables

The above discussion has admitted uncertainty only in the sales volume variable. However, the selling price, variable cost and fixed cost may also be uncertain. This gives rise to a particular problem as the *product* of two or more independent and normally distributed random variables is not necessarily a normally distributed random variable. For instance, if the sales volume and selling price for a particular product are independent normally distributed random variables, the profit function will be normally distributed only under extremely restrictive assumptions. Some writers have attempted to overcome this problem by using alternative distributions for the selling price and sales volume variables, or by using approximations to derive a profit distribution. However, such statistical work has either resulted in models which are subject to very restrictive assumptions or to models which are extremely complex. Statistical analysis of situations in which the selling price and sales volume are not independent appears to be almost impossible at the present time.

Simulation has been suggested as an alternative to statistical methods for deriving the parameters of a profit distribution. Two methods have been suggested, direct simulation and model simulation. Direct simulation involves constructing a model which describes the relationship between profit and all the underlying variables. Simulation techniques are used to select values for each variable and hence to determine profit. Successive repetitions of the simulation can give rise to a range of profit figures which indicate the nature of the profit distribution. In a practical problem such an approach is likely to need vast computing facilities, if it is to be done reliably. Unfortunately it is not possible to determine an appropriate sample size (i.e., number of repetitions) using available statistical techniques, thus the 'accuracy' of the resulting profit distribution cannot be assessed.

The alternative of model simulation has the advantage of requiring rather less computing facilities. This approach involves two stages. In the first stage small simulations are run to determine the mean and standard deviations of each of the underlying variables. These parameters are then used in a larger simulation model to determine the parameters of the profit function.

Simulation techniques may be more acceptable to practitioners as they involve rather less analytic ability, although model simulation does require knowledge of statistical distributions. But both methods require considerable computing facilities and are subject to unknown sampling errors. Neither appears to be widely used in practice.

5.8 Some Final Points

The various approaches to C–V–P analysis described above make no explicit statement about the underlying decision models. Following the early research of Jaedicke and Robichek, a knowledge of the distribution of profits in terms of their mean, variance (or standard deviation) and possibly higher order moments, is assumed to be useful to the decision maker. However, Magee (1975) pointed out that under the normal assumptions of the capital asset pricing model it is the covariance of profit with the return on the market portfolio which is important for the decision maker. Thus, the form of C–V–P analysis may be contingent upon the manager's decision model. Much of the research in this area appears to be based on a simple extension of the economic model described in Chapter 2. In the certainty model, profit was shown to be important and C–V–P researchers appear to have reasoned that the distribution of profits must, therefore, be important under conditions of uncertainty. However, the introduction of uncertainty may, itself, alter the underlying decision model.

Although C–V–P researchers in the early 1970s did not make their decision models explicit, the analytical techniques that they used owed much to statistical decision theory. Decision theory terms, such as random variables, expected value and variance were commonly observed in the C–V–P literature at that time. The investigation of variances literature went somewhat further than the C–V–P literature and explicitly used decision models expressed in decision theory terms. Chapter 6 will discuss some of the decision theory approaches to the investigation of variances.

Before leaving C–V–P analysis it is relevant to consider the likely implementation problems. In this chapter some of the simpler statistical techniques for handling uncertainty in C–V–P analysis were illustrated. To take the analysis further and to relax some of the more restrictive assumptions requires a considerable knowledge of statistics. Such knowledge may be beyond the average accountant and manager in practice. Nevertheless, if these techniques were thought to be valuable, the services of a statistician could be purchased. Even if this were the case, it is likely that the set-up costs of the models would be quite high, not just in terms of the statistician's time, but also in terms of the managerial effort which would be required in order to provide reliable estimates for the statistical models. The running costs of these models could be quite low, unless a very extensive range of products is produced, in which case vast data inputs would be required and the complexity of the models would necessitate considerable computing capacity. Finally, the available empirical evidence suggests that extensions of C–V–P analysis for uncertainty are not widely used in practice although the simple deterministic version of C–V–P analysis is a commonly used tool of the financial manager.

Variance Investigation Models 6

It was suggested at the end of Chapter 5 that statistical decision theory had an impact on research in the area of C–V–P analysis. Another area where decision theory had an important impact was in the investigation of variances. All business planning, whether in the form of budgets or standards, is based on estimates of prices, volumes, costs, etc., and any outcome can only be expected to approximate these estimates. Outcomes will not necessarily equal the original estimates, even if the estimates were 'accurate' and the process has been 'under control'. Some variation around the estimate or expected outcome is inevitable. Thus, when a variance is reported, the manager should ask whether it represents a significant deviation from the budget or whether it is simply a random fluctuation around the expected outcome. Variance investigation models are concerned with decisions to investigate the cause of particular variances and in particular, to distinguish significant deviations from random fluctuations.

A simple decision theory model for the investigation of variances was introduced into the accounting literature early in the 1960s by Bierman *et al.* (1961). Although substantially refined models were proposed in the statistical and management science literatures, it was not until the end of that decade that major developments appeared in the accounting literature. These developments coincided with the use of statistical decision theory to introduce uncertainty into the decision models favoured by management accounting researchers.

6.1   The Decision Theory Approach

The decision theory approach dictates that an investigation should be undertaken when the expected cost of the investigation is less than the expected cost of not investigating. For this purpose, the cost of not investigating comprises the loss of the benefit which would be obtained through investigating and correcting the cause of the variance. In very simple terms, the costs and benefits of investigation can be set out in a pay-off matrix, as illustrated in Table 6.1. It is assumed that a particular variance has been observed and that a decision must be taken either to investigate or not to investigate its causes.

TABLE 6.1
Cost/Benefit of Investigation

	States		Expected value
	In control (p)	Out of control $(1 - p)$	Expected value
Investigate	$-C$	$B-C$	$-pC+(1-p)(B-C)$
Don't investigate	0	0	0

In this illustration two mutually exclusive states are possible. First, the underlying system may be 'in control' and the variance simply a random fluctuation around the expected outcome. The second possible state is that the system is, in some way, 'out of control', i.e., it is not proceeding according to plan. If the system is in fact out of control, corrective action may be taken. It is assumed that such action will result in a benefit of B. This benefit could represent the cost saving which will arise through bringing the system back under control and thereby avoiding variances in future periods. However, a cost of C will be incurred when an investigation is undertaken.

Now consider the two rows of Table 6.1. If no investigation takes place (represented by the second row), no cost will be incurred nor benefit obtained, whatever the state of the system. If an investigation is undertaken (represented by the first row), but shows the system to be in control, there will be a net outflow of the investigation cost, C. Alternatively, if the investigation shows the system to be out of control, there will be a net benefit of B less the investigation cost of C.

The expected values of the two possible actions can be calculated using the probabilities that, on the one hand, the system is still in control and on the other hand, that it is out of control. For this purpose the probabilities are expressed in terms which reflect the fact that a particular variance has been observed. For the present, assume that the probability that the system is still in control can be denoted by p (methods of determining this probability will be discussed later). The probability that the system is out of control will, accordingly, be $(1 - p)$. The expected values of investigation and no investigation are shown at the extreme right-hand side of Table 6.1.

The investigation should be undertaken if:

$$-pC + (1-p)(B-C) > 0 \qquad (6.1)$$

or rearranging:

$$C < B(1-p) \qquad (6.2)$$

The latter expression indicates that the investigation should take place if the cost of investigation, C, is less than the benefit to be obtained from correcting an out of control system, B, multiplied by the probability that the system is out of control. The loss of this expected benefit, $B\,(1-p)$, represents the opportunity cost of not investigating. Thus, equation (6.2) restates the decision theory criterion mentioned earlier – investigate if the expected cost of the investigation is less than the expected cost of not investigating.

The relationship expressed in equations (6.1) and (6.2) can be simplified to provide a critical ratio of the form:

$$\frac{B-C}{B} > p \qquad\qquad (6.3)$$

An investigation should take place if the ratio of the net benefit, $B-C$, to the gross benefit, B, exceeds the probability that the system is still in control. For instance, assume that a variance of £55 implies a 0.15 probability that the system is still in control. If the gross benefit, B, is £100 and the cost of investigation, C, is £60, then the critical ratio of net benefit to gross benefit is 40/100 = 0.4. Thus, the investigation should take place as 0.4 is greater than 0.15.

This relatively simple analysis begs numerous questions. In particular, how are B and C to be estimated and more importantly, how can we determine p – the probability that the system is still in control, given a variance has been observed?

6.2 Determining Probabilities

The paper by Bierman *et al.* (1961) suggested that the necessary probabilities for a variance investigation decision could be determined by computing the probability that a particular observation, such as a variance, comes from the null (in control) distribution. For instance, suppose expected costs for a department were £1 000 with a standard deviation of £200, while actual costs of £1 400 are recorded. Figure 6.1 represents the assumed probability distribution of the department's costs when they are under control. The mean of the distribution, which is assumed to be normal, is £1 000 and its standard deviation is £200. The actual costs of £1 400 exceed the mean of the distribution by two standard deviations. A table of areas under the normal distribution indicates that there is only about a $2\frac{1}{2}$ per cent chance that an observation from that distribution will occur at least two standard deviations above the mean. Thus, it could be concluded that there is only a 0.025

FIGURE 6.1
A Simple Probability Distribution

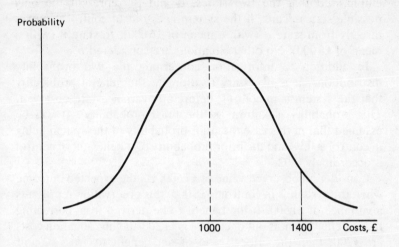

probability that the system is still in control, given that costs of £1 400 (which represent a variance of £400) have been recorded.

Other writers have criticised this approach because it ignores prior information – such as the variances recorded in previous periods and managers' subjective estimates of the probabilities that the system is in control or out of control. Various alternative methods have been suggested. For purposes of illustration, one such approach will be described in this chapter. The approach illustrated is one of the least complex methods to appear in the literature. The difficulties and complexities of some of the alternatives are discussed later.

6.3 An Illustration

To begin, it is necessary to assume that there are only two possible states for the underlying system. The first state, α, represents the system in control. In this state the expected value of the outcome distribution (e.g., total costs for the month) is £6 000 and the standard deviation is £500. The alternative state, β, represents the system out of control, in which case the expected outcome is £8 000 and the outcome distribution has a standard deviation of £500. It is emphasised that the two states, α and β, represent the only possible states. Thus, if the system goes out of control it moves directly from state α (with a mean of £6 000), to state β (with a mean of £8 000). No other situations are considered.

In addition to information concerning the two probability distributions, it is necessary to estimate the general probability that the system is in control, before any variances are observed. This probability is known as 'the prior probability'. It will be assumed that in this case the prior probability of the system being in control is 0.98 and the prior probability of it being out of control is accordingly 0.02.

Consider an observed value of £7 500. As the expected outcome when the system is in control is £6 000, this observation represents a variance of £1 500. If the benefit to be derived from correcting the system when it is out of control is £1 200 and investigation costs are £200, then the critical ratio of net benefit to gross benefit (equation (6.3)) is 1 000/1 200, or 0.83. The variance should be investigated if the probability that the system is still in control, given that a variance of £1 500 has been observed, is less than this critical ratio.

This illustration was devised by Dyckman (1969) who objected to the omission of prior probabilities in the work of Bierman *et al*. Dyckman proposed using Bayes' theorem to combine the new information given by the variance and the prior probability that the system is in control. The use of Bayes' theorem is illustrated below.

6.4 Bayes' Theorem

Bayes' theorem is a statistical technique for revising prior probabilities to reflect new information. In the present context, it can be used to determine the probability that the system is still in control, given that a particular variance has been observed. The general form of Bayes' theorem can be written as:

$$\Pr(X|V) = \frac{\Pr(V|X)\,\Pr(X)}{\Pr(V)} \qquad\qquad (6.4)$$

The term $\Pr(X|V)$ is the probability of X occurring, given that V has been observed. For purposes of the present discussion, X can be regarded as a particular state of the world (such as the system being in control) and V can be regarded as the observation of a particular variance. Bayes' theorem states that the probability of X, given V, equals the probability of V, given X (e.g., the probability of observing a variance of V, given that the system is in control) multiplied by the prior probability of X (e.g., the prior probability that the system is in control) divided by the probability of observing V.

The two distributions described earlier are illustrated in Figure 6.2. Both distributions have a standard deviation of £500, but the mean of α is £6000 while the mean of β is £8000. There is a probability of costs of £7500 on each distribution. The observation of £7500 is three standard deviations from the mean of the α distribution and one standard deviation from the mean of the β distribution.

FIGURE 6.2
Probability Distribution for States α and β

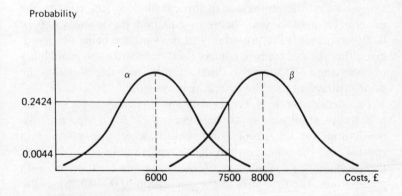

A table of the ordinates of a normal density function indicates the probabilities of values occurring at particular points, measured in terms of standard deviations from the mean of the normal distribution. In other words, this table indicates the height of the normal distribution at each particular point (rather than the more usual area under the curve). Reference to such a table discloses that the probability of observing a value which is one standard deviation from the mean of a normal distribution is 0.2424 and the probability of a point being three standard deviations from the mean is 0.0044. To summarise:

The probability of observing a value of £7 500 is:
0.0044 if the system is in control, and 0.2424 if the system is out of control.

Bayes' theorem can now be used to determine the probabilities of the system being either in control, or out of control, given that a variance has been observed. The probability that the system is still in control can be expressed as follows (the detail of the calculation is explained below):

Pr(in control|variance of £1 500)

$$= \frac{0.0044(0.98)}{0.0044(0.98)+0.2424(0.02)}$$
$$= 0.47 \qquad (6.5)$$

Consider first the numerator of this calculation. Referring to the general form of Bayes' theorem, equation (6.4), the value of 0.0044 represents the probability of the variance being observed, given that the system is in control (in other words, the probability of observing £7 500 on the α distribution). The value of 0.98 is the prior probability that the system is in control.

The denominator of the calculation in equation (6.5) is the probability of observing an outcome of £7 500. There are two possibilities for this observation. One is when the system is in control, and the other is when the system is out of control. Thus, the probability of observing £7 500 is the combination of both possibilities. The first term in the calculation, 0.0044(0.98), is the probability of observing £7 500 on the in control (α) distribution, multiplied by the prior probability of that distribution. The second term, 0.2424(0.02), is the probability of observing £7 500 on the out of control (β) distribution, multiplied by the probability of that distribution. The sum of these two terms indicates the probability of costs of £7 500 being observed.

The result of the calculation in equation (6.5) indicates that the probability that the system is still in control, given that a variance of £1 500 has been observed, is 0.47. We calculated earlier that the variance should be investigated if the probability that the system is still in control, given the variance, is less than the critical ratio of net benefits to gross benefits, i.e., 0.83. As 0.47 is less than 0.83, the variance should be investigated.

In order to complete the calculations, more out of interest than necessity, the probability that the system is out of control, given the variance of £1 500, can also be calculated. Once again using Bayes' theorem:

Pr(out of control|variance of £1 500)

$$= \frac{0.2424(0.02)}{0.0044(0.98) + 0.2424(0.02)}$$

$$= 0.53 \tag{6.6}$$

The reader is invited to confirm each of the figures in this equation – they are the 'out of control' equivalents of the figures in equation (6.5). This second calculation indicates that the probability that the system is out of control, given that the variance of £1 500 has been observed, is 0.53. As only two states are considered in the illustration, the probabilities that the system is in control, 0.47, and out of control, 0.53, should sum to unity. This provides a useful check on the calculations.

To conclude this illustration the steps which were taken in the variance investigation decision are summarised as follows. First, the critical ratio of net benefits to gross benefits of investigation was calculated. Bayes' theorem was then used to compute the probability that the system is still in control, given that the variance has been observed. The variance should be investigated if the probability that the system is still in control is less than the critical ratio of net benefits to gross benefits. Bayes' theorem was also used to compute the probability that the system is out of control. This provided a check on the calculations, as the sum of the probabilities that the system is in control and out of control should be unity.

6.5 Discussion

The method of analysis described above can be used to determine the probability that the system is still in control, given that a variance has been observed. It extends the analysis beyond the very simple case discussed by Bierman *et al.* (1961), but it is a long way from being a realistic model of the factors likely to be involved in practice. For instance, in most practical situations there will be more than two discrete states of the world. In addition, the decision rules discussed above are very naive in their treatment of the costs and benefits arising from investigation and correction. There are likely to be dynamic relationships between current actions and future benefits, but these are ignored in the simple models. For instance, if no action is taken this period, the system could simply revert to an in control situation next period or could go further out of control and increase the loss caused by not investigating. Furthermore, even if corrective actions are taken it is not certain that benefits will actually accrue – it may be impossible to correct the factors which have taken the system out of control.

A number of papers have attempted to overcome some of the apparent shortcomings of the simple models. These papers used several techniques, at various levels of complexity. Nevertheless, theoretical problems remain and variance investigation models are still a subject for discussion in the academic literature. The important point which emerges from an examination of this literature, especially the literature of the early 1970s, is that researchers at that time were attempting to relax the assumptions of the simple models in the belief that they were making the analysis more 'realistic'. The implied assumption was that the most appropriate model is the one which gets closest to the reality of decision making in practice.

This attempt to develop more 'realistic' models had a parallel in the work on C–V–P analysis which was discussed in the previous chapter. In fact, researchers in a number of areas of management accounting attempted, during the early years of the 1970s, to relax the certainty assumptions of earlier models by introducing uncertainty in the form of probability distributions into their work, apparently in an attempt to make the analysis more realistic. Nevertheless, these extensions did not represent a fundamental change in the underlying economic framework which dictated the direction of much management accounting research at that time. The framework described in Chapter 2 continued to have an important impact. The decision maker was still assumed to have available at no cost all the information he/she required to arrive at a deterministic solution to his/her decision problem. But instead of certainty, the information was assumed to be expressed in the form of known probability distributions. These decision models were intended to assist the decision maker to utilise probabilistic information in deciding on a particular course of action, such as whether or not to investigate a particular variance.

In common with researchers in other areas of management accounting in the late 1960s and early 1970s, the researchers who developed complex models for variance investigations did not explore the difficulties and costs involved in obtaining the information which would be required to implement their models in practice, nor were the problems likely to be faced by decision makers implementing the models given serious consideration. However, by the middle of the 1970s some writers were beginning to become concerned about such problems. For instance, Magee (1976) used a simulation model to evaluate the relative usefulness of simple and complex variance investigation models. His paper will be described in more detail in Chapter 9, but at this point it is interesting to note that Magee concluded that simple models may be the most useful in practice.

The illustrations of C–V–P analysis and cost variance investigation models in Chapter 5 and this chapter indicate that during the early years of the 1970s, management accounting researchers were using decision theory models to explore the effects of uncertainty on the conventional subject matter of management accounting. In addition, the effects of uncertainty were explored in other areas, such as human resource accounting, budgeting and inventory control. But as mentioned above, the analysis of expected costs and benefits in decision theory terms represents only a minor change in the economic framework which underlies management accounting's conventional wisdom. The analysis still belongs to the conditional truth approach to management accounting.

Dyckman (1975) argued that although managers have been thinking in decision theory terms for much longer than formal methods have been available, statistical decision theory is not descriptive; it is normative. It attempts to find rigorous methods which 'ought' to be used by decision makers to incorporate costs, benefits and uncertainty into their decision making. As pointed out in Chapter 3, these methods have not been widely adopted in practice. Many reasons can be suggested to account for this, including the belief that such methods are too costly to implement, as compared to their perceived benefits.

Under conditions of certainty the decision maker is assumed to have available all the information he/she needs – at no cost. The questions to be answered concern the use of this information in arriving at decisions. The task facing researchers is to construct the decision model/method to be used by decision makers. When uncertainty is introduced into the analysis, however, questions concerning the cost and value of information become important. The provision of information can reduce the uncertainty of a decision-making situation. But information is a costly good and its production can be evaluated in terms of costs and benefits. The advances in C–V–P analysis and investigation of variance models in the 1970s, described in this and the previous chapter, tended to ignore information costs. As a result, the proposed techniques became more and more complex as researchers attempted to be more 'realistic' in their modelling of decision-making situations.

Under the conditional truth approach, which was typical of management accounting research in the 1950s and 1960s, the provision of information is assumed to follow unproblematically from the decision model. When uncertainty was introduced into decision models in the early 1970s, this assumption was not challenged, and decision models became very complex. The aim of such research was to develop ideal models for decision-making, but the costs and benefits of information were not explicitly considered. The next two chapters will first illustrate a means of valuing information in decision theory terms and then describe information economics as a means of formally examining the provision of information.

The introduction of information economics into management accounting research in the middle of the 1970s represented a departure from the conditional truth approach and a first step towards the development of an alternative 'costly truth' approach (Demski and Feltham, 1976). In this alternative approach information production costs are explicitly considered in examining decision models. The provision of information is regarded as problematic and the selection of information and decision model are analysed together.

Before completing this chapter, some comments are needed about the contribution to the literature made by researchers who attempted to extend the simple economic framework described in Chapter 2 by introducing uncertainty expressed in terms of known probability distributions. These researchers demonstrated the limitations of certainty models and the complex nature of uncertainty in business decision making. In attempting to develop ideal (or realistic) models, they introduced an extreme level of complexity into their analysis. This highlighted the need for an examination of information costs in management accounting models. As such these attempts at providing ideal models made a useful contribution in their time.

Papers which continue to strive for reality in decision models without adequate attention to implementation problems and information costs may have rather less value, however. In this context, a distinction can be drawn between the models which are proposed for use by managers and/or accountants in practice on a day-to-day basis and the models used by academics and consultants to analyse decision-making situations. The latter models could be very complex as researchers could be trained in the necessary statistical and decision theory techniques and have the time to devote to the development of such models. Researchers could use their models to analyse practical situations and to make recommendations concerning the techniques (or models) which might be useful in practice. Unless the researchers' models are sufficiently complex to incorporate notions of information costs and benefits, they are unlikely to provide valid prescriptions for practice. But, once information costs and benefits are integrated into the analysis, it may be possible to identify the role of 'simple' models in practice. The choice between simple and complex management accounting techniques (including variance investigations models) will be examined further in Chapter 9. In the meantime, a method for valuing information will be described.

III

Information Costs
and Benefits

Value of Information

7

As argued at the end of Chapter 6, many of the decision models developed by accounting researchers, especially in the early 1970s, ignored information costs. Although researchers attempted to relax many of the assumptions which were made, either implicitly or explicitly, in developing the models that formed the basis of management accounting's conventional wisdom, the assumption of costless information remained intact for some time. In seeking to realistically model decision-making situations, researchers introduced considerable complexity into their models and created a potential demand for vast amounts of information. Neither the difficulties of obtaining such information, nor the associated costs were explicitly recognised in many of the models. However, in practice information is not costless.

7.1 Information Costs

Information can be obtained from various sources, but many of these are costly. The most obvious example of an information source is the accounting system. Accountants, book-keepers, clerks have to be paid in order to produce the information; office space has to be provided; furniture, calculating machines and computers have to be purchased. In addition, opportunity costs may be incurred in providing the managerial inputs into the accounting system. For instance, managers may have to devote a substantial amount of their time to preparing estimates to be included in budgets. The time spent preparing these estimates could be used for direct supervision of productive activities. In addition to the internal costs of providing information, there are also external costs which may be incurred. For instance, market research consultants may be employed to provide information for marketing decisions; consulting engineers may be used for particularly difficult production decisions; subscriptions may be paid for market intelligence; and so on. Thus, there is great variety in the nature of information costs.

The question that will be addressed in this chapter is whether it is worth acquiring a particular information source. But as will become clearer later, information can be evaluated only in the context of a particular decision or set of decisions. In general, a decision maker would not want to pay more for information than the value to the business of having that information. Accordingly, the value of information must be assessed in the context of the specific decisions which have to be taken.

There are two related approaches to problems concerning the acquisition of information. The first involves asking the question, 'Is it worth acquiring information from a particular source at a given cost?'. The second involves calculating the maximum amount that it would be worth paying to acquire information from a particular source, and then comparing this maximum amount with the actual cost which would be incurred. In this second case, the information should be acquired if the actual cost is less than the maximum amount the decision maker would be willing to pay. As will be explained below both these approaches involve evaluating the effects of information on particular decisions.

The value of information can be determined by comparing the decision outcome which is expected if the information is acquired, against the outcome expected in the absence of the information. In this chapter, decision outcomes will be evaluated in terms of expected values. Such evaluations ignore the decision maker's attitude to risk (or at least, assume that the decision maker is risk neutral). This approach is used here purely for ease of presentation. If the decision maker's subjective expected utility for particular outcomes can be identified the analysis could be undertaken in utility terms. In Chapter 8, when information economics is discussed, the approaches adopted in this chapter will be generalised and the case of a subjective expected utility maximiser will be considered. But for the present, it will be sufficient to assume that the decision maker wants to maximise expected values.

7.2   The Value of Information

Two approaches for evaluating particular sources of information were mentioned above. The first approach is concerned only with the cost of the information, i.e., whether it is worth acquiring at a given cost. The second approach, however, is concerned with the maximum amount that the decision maker would be prepared to pay for a particular information source. The maximum amount can be regarded as the value of the information to the decision maker. Both these approaches are illustrated below with the aid of a simple example.

Consider the decision to buy one or other of two machines. The first machine is relatively small and most suited to meet a low level of demand for the products it produces, whereas the second machine is considerably larger and most suited to a high level of demand. If the larger machine is acquired and the demand is low, a loss would be incurred. The net present values of each machine in the two possible demand situations (low demand and high demand) are set out in Table 7.1 in the form of a pay-off table.

The two demand situations are assumed to be equally likely. Thus as the pay-off table indicates, the probability of the demand situation occurring is 0.5 in each case. The expected value of acquiring each machine can be calculated by multiplying the pay-off from each demand situation by its probability. The expected value of the small machine is £80(0.5)+£120(0.5)=£100. A similar calculation produces the expected value of £50 for the large machine. In these circumstances, without further information about the likely demand, the expected value will be at a maximum of £100 if the small machine is purchased.

TABLE 7.1
Pay-off Table

Expected outcomes (NPV in £s)	Demand		Expected value
	Low (Pr=0.5)	High (Pr=0.5)	
Small machine	80	120	100
Large machine	−100	200	50

Now, consider the possibility of a market research survey which, at a cost of £20, could give a perfect prediction of the level of demand. In other words, if market research predicts a low level of demand, the probability of demand being low will be 1.0 and the probability of the demand being high will be 0. Similar, but reversed, probabilities apply if market research predicts a high level of demand.

As a result of the market research information the size of machine can be matched with the level of demand. Thus, if demand is predicted to be low a small machine will be purchased, whereas if demand is predicted to be high a large machine will be purchased. The resulting net present values will be £60 for a predicted low demand and £180 for a predicted high demand. These figures were calculated by taking the highest net present value in the case of the low demand and high demand respectively and deducting the costs of the market research, £20.

When the decision to commission a market research survey has to be taken, it is not known whether a high or a low demand will be predicted. Therefore, the best estimate of the outcome of the market research is a 50 per cent chance that it will predict a low demand and a 50 per cent chance that it will predict a high demand – as these are the probabilities which are currently associated with high and low demand. Assuming the market research survey is undertaken, the expected value of the decision can be computed by summing the outcomes which would follow each possible prediction multiplied by the probability of that prediction. In the above illustration, the expected value is £120, i.e., £180(0.5) + £60(0.5).

The two decision-making situations can now be compared. The expected value of the decision without the market research survey is £100, while the expected value with the market research survey (including the cost of that survey) is £120. The preferred course of action, specifically the action which maximises expected value, is to undertake the market research survey. Thus, the information should be acquired. This implies that the value of the information exceeds its costs, otherwise it would not be acquired. An alternative approach is to measure the value of information directly, as will be described below.

The value of information can be computed by evaluating the maximum expected value of the decision without additional information, and then comparing the result with the maximum expected value with the further information (but ignoring the costs of that information). In the above simple example, it was demonstrated that the maximum expected value without the information which would be provided by a market research survey was £100. If the cost of the survey is ignored, the maximum net present values which can be obtained with the information will be £80 if the small machine is acquired and £200 if the large machine is acquired.

At the decision stage (i.e., before any market research is undertaken) the expected value of the decision with the market research information can be computed as follows: £80(0.5) + £200(0.5) = £140. Thus, the market research survey increases the maximum expected value from £100 to £140. The difference between these two expected values represents the maximum amount that should be paid for the information. Thus, £40 is the value of the market research information in this particular decision-making situation. As demonstrated above, at a cost of £20, the information should be acquired – as the cost is less than the value of the information.

In the above illustration, it was assumed that the market research survey will give a 100 per cent accurate prediction of the expected demand. Such accuracy in information is unlikely in practice. Although information may give a clearer picture of expected outcomes, it is unlikely to give perfect predictions. As might be expected, the value of perfect information will always be greater than the value of imperfect information, except when both equal zero. The value of information (whether perfect or imperfect) would be zero in a situation where the information would not change the decision. For instance, in the case of the above illustration, if the small machine was preferred irrespective of whether the demand is high or low, information concerning the expected demand would have no value.

Methods for evaluating imperfect information are similar to those described above. But with imperfect information it is more difficult to revise the probability estimates of particular outcomes to reflect the new information. A further illustration is set out below to describe the process by which imperfect information can be valued.

7.3   An Ice-cream Manufacturer

The illustration which will be used to demonstrate the valuation of imperfect information follows the second of the two approaches described earlier. That is, it values the information in terms of the maximum amount which should be paid to acquire it. Consider an ice-cream manufacturer who makes ice-cream daily in tubs. Any batch not sold at the end of the day is regarded as a total loss, but there is no loss of goodwill if demand is not met. In general, the demand depends on the weather. Past experience suggests that for the present time of the year the likely daily demand can be expressed as follows:

Demand	Probability
1 tub	0.1
2 tubs	0.5
3 tubs	0.4

For simplicity it is assumed that only whole tubs will be sold. The cost of producing a tub of ice-cream is £80 and the revenue generated by the sale thereof is £100.

Table 7.2 summarises the decision problem in the absence of any further information. The pay-off table indicates the contribution that is earned from a combination of each level of production

TABLE 7.2
Decision Without Information

Pay-off table	Actual demand		
(Contribution earned in £s)	1	2	3
Production 1 tub	20	20	20
Production 2 tubs	(60)	40	40
Production 3 tubs	(140)	(40)	60

Expected value table (£s)	Actual demand			
	1	2	3	Expected
	0.1	0.5	0.4	value
Production 1 tub	2	10	8	20
Production 2 tubs	(6)	20	16	30
Production 3 tubs	(14)	(20)	24	(10)

and each possible level of demand. If 1 tub is produced per day, then 1 tub will be the maximum that can be sold. The contribution of £20 (sales revenue of £100 minus variable cost of £80) will be earned irrespective of whether the demand is 1, 2 or 3 tubs. If 2 tubs are produced a maximum contribution of £40 can be earned provided the demand is either 2 or 3 tubs. If only 1 tub is sold, when 2 tubs have been produced, a loss of £60 will be incurred – sales revenue of £100 less variable cost of £160. If 3 tubs are produced the maximum contribution of £60 (3 × £20 per tub) will be earned only when 3 tubs are actually demanded. Losses will be incurred if the demand is only 1 or 2 tubs. The reader is encouraged to work through the calculations of the loss incurred in each of these cases to confirm the remaining figures in the pay-off table.

The expected value table in the second part of Table 7.2 is computed by multiplying each element of the pay-off table by the probability that the actual demand will be achieved. For instance, the element at the top left-hand corner, which represents production of 1 tub and actual demand of 1 tub, is calculated by taking the £20 from the pay-off table and multiplying it by 0.1 – the probability of demand actually being 1 tub. The expected value of each level of production can then be computed by adding across each of the rows. The table indicates that the expected value will be maximised if 2 tubs are produced daily.

Similar calculations can be performed using a decision tree – see illustration in Figure 7.1. On a decision tree a rectangular box indicates a decision and a circle represents an uncertain event, the outcome of which is usually termed a state of the world. In the

FIGURE 7.1
Decision Tree Approach

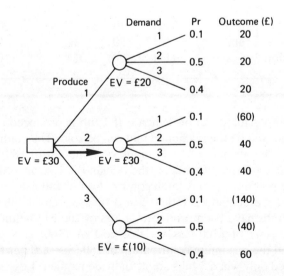

ice-cream manufacturer's problem, the decision involves producing 1, 2 or 3 tubs. This gives rise to three branches from the rectangular box on the left-hand side of the decision tree. On each of these branches there is a circle which represents the uncertain demand. This uncertainty concerning demand gives rise to three branches – one each for the possible demands of 1, 2 or 3 tubs. At the end of these branches is the outcome and its probability. For instance, if we consider producing 1 tub and the demand is 1 tub, then the outcome will be £20 with a probability of 0.1. The other outcomes and associated probabilities can be interpreted in the same way.

The expected value of each production decision can be calculated by multiplying the outcome and the probability for each state of the world, e.g., following the branch indicating the production of 1 tub, the expected value is 20(0.1) + 20(0.5) + 20(0.4) = £20. The other two expected values, associated with the production of 2 and 3 tubs, are £30, and £(10) respectively. These are the same expected values as were calculated in Table 7.2. Thus, the decision is to produce 2 tubs daily, as this generates the maximum expected value of £30. The arrow on Figure 7.1 indicates this decision.

Before considering imperfect information, it will be helpful to calculate the value of perfect information. For the time being, assume that perfect weather forecasts can be provided. These forecasts will enable the ice-cream manufacturer to make accurate predictions of the actual demand. Thus, following the receipt of a weather forecast for a particular day the probability of one level of demand for that day will be 1.0 and the probability of the other two levels will be zero. Given such perfect predictions of the actual demand day by day, the ice-cream manufacturer will be able to select the best level of production to meet the demand each and every day.

The pay-off table in Table 7.2 indicates that if the predicted demand is 1 tub the best production level is also 1 tub. Similarly, if 2 tubs are predicted then 2 tubs should be produced and if 3 tubs are predicted, 3 tubs should be produced. Remember that in this case the predictions are assumed to be perfect and that if, for instance, 3 tubs are predicted, then the actual demand will be 3 tubs. Thus, given information concerning the weather, optimum production decisions can be taken.

At the time the decision maker is considering the acquisition of information (in the form of weather forecasts), he/she cannot tell what the forecast will be for any particular day. However, he/she can estimate the likelihood of each of the three levels of demand. Therefore, the expected value of the decision, given that perfect information can be calculated:

$$EV(\text{with perfect information})$$
$$= £20(0.1) + £40(0.5) + £60(0.4) = £46 \qquad (7.1)$$

Thus, the decision situation has an expected value of £46, if perfect information is available. This represents an increase of £16 (i.e., £46−£30) over the maximum expected value without the further information. Accordingly, the value of this perfect information is £16. This is the maximum amount which the ice-cream manufacturer would be willing to pay per day for a perfect weather forecast – that is, one which is totally reliable.

7.4 The Value of Imperfect Information

We can now proceed to consider the value of imperfect information. Let us say that the forecasts concerning the weather provide demand predictions which are only 80 per cent reliable. In other words, if the actual demand is, say, 2 tubs there is a 0.8 probability that a demand of 2 tubs will be predicted, but there is also a 0.2 probability that a demand of either 1 tub or 3 tubs will be predicted. Let us assume that in the latter case the probability of 1 tub being predicted is 0.1 and the probability of 3 tubs being predicted is also 0.1. To explore the implications of this imperfect information we can look at the likely predictions for, say, 100 days. Table 7.3 illustrates the reliability of the information over such a period.

Each element of the matrix set out in Table 7.3 represents the number of days, out of a total of 100, when the particular combination of prediction and actual demand will occur, if the imperfect information is acquired. For example, the top left-hand element indicates that on 8 days out of the 100 the prediction will be 1 tub and the actual demand will also be 1 tub; whereas the next element on the top row indicates that on 5 days out of the 100 the prediction will be 1 tub, but the actual demand will be 2 tubs. The other elements can be interpreted in a similar way. The particular figures in the matrix were built up as follows.

As already indicated, the probabilities of the actual demand being 1, 2 or 3 tubs are 0.1, 0.5 and 0.4 respectively. Thus, in a period of 100 days there will be, on average, 10 days when the demand is 1 tub, 50 days when the demand is 2 tubs, and 40 days when the demand is 3 tubs. These figures are entered as the bottom line of Table 7.3.

TABLE 7.3
Reliability of Information

No. of days matrix	Actual demand			
	1	2	3	Total
Prediction 1	8	5	4	17
Prediction 2	1	40	4	45
Prediction 3	1	5	32	38
	10	50	40	100

Next, consider the 10 days when the actual demand is 1 tub. Because the information provided by the weather forecasts is only 80 per cent reliable it is to be expected that on 8 of these 10 days 1 tub will be predicted, while on 1 day 2 tubs will be predicted and on 1 day 3 tubs will be predicted. These figures (8, 1 and 1) can be entered in the first column of the matrix. Similarly, looking at the 50 days when the demand is actually 2 tubs; on 40 of these days 2 tubs will be predicted, but 1 tub will be predicted on 5 days, and 3 tubs will be predicted on a further 5 days. These figures form the second column of the matrix. Similar calculations can be made for the 40 days on which the actual demand is 3 tubs – the third column.

Finally, the figures on the rows are added across the matrix. These figures now indicate the number of days when each of the three predictions will be made. Out of the 100 days, 1 tub will be predicted on 17 occasions. On 8 of these days the demand will actually be 1 tub, on 5 of these days the demand will actually be 2 tubs, and on 4 of these days the demand will be 3 tubs. Thus, given a prediction of 1 tub, the probability of the actual demand being 1 tub is 8/17ths, while the probabilities of the demand being 2 and 3 tubs are 5/17ths and 4/17ths respectively. These are the revised probabilities which apply if there is a prediction of 1 tub. The probabilities of the actual demand being 1, 2 and 3 tubs, given a prediction of 2 tubs, are 1/45th, 40/45ths and 4/45ths respectively. Finally, the probabilities, given a prediction of 3 tubs, are 1/38th, 5/38ths and 32/38ths respectively.

To summarise, Table 7.3 describes the revision of probabilities to reflect the imperfect information. Originally, the probabilities of 1, 2 and 3 tubs being demanded were 0.1, 0.5 and 0.4, but these probabilities can be revised to reflect the new information provided by the weather forecasts. For instance, if this information predicts a demand of 1 tub, the revised probabilities will be 8/17ths, 5/17ths and 4/17ths. It will be demonstrated in Chapter 8 that these probability revisions follow Bayes' theorem. But for the present it is sufficient to consider the effect of the information on a representative 100 days.

As the ice-cream manufacturer has the choice of proceeding with information or without information, he/she has two decisions to make. The first decision is whether or not to buy the information. He/she then has to decide the level of production. The expected value of the decision to proceed without further information has already been calculated. In that case, the expected value was £30. The decision tree which led to that value was illustrated in Figure 7.1. A partial view of the decision tree for the expanded problem, with the possibility of information, is illustrated in Figure 7.2

The box at the extreme left-hand side of Figure 7.2 represents the choice of whether or not to buy the information. If no information is acquired the expected value is £30. This part of the decision tree is not shown in detail in order to keep the presentation as simple as possible. If the information is acquired, however, there is still the uncertainty concerning the prediction which will be made. The weather forecast could lead to one of three possible predictions. The probabilities of these predictions were determined in Table 7.3. The column at the extreme

FIGURE 7.2
Using a Decision Tree

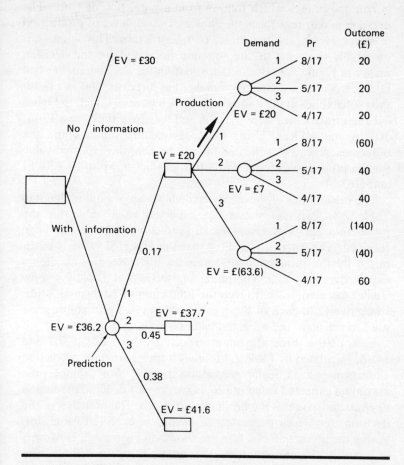

right-hand side of the table indicates the likelihood of each of the three predictions being made. On 17 of the representative 100 days, a demand of 1 tub was predicted, while on a further 45 days the prediction was 2 tubs, and on the remaining 38 days the prediction was 3 tubs. The number of days, out of the total of 100, indicates the probability of each prediction; namely, 0.17, 0.45 and 0.38 for predictions of 1, 2 and 3 tubs respectively.

Returning to Figure 7.2, the probabilities of the three predictions are entered on the branches of the decision tree emerging from the circle which represents the uncertain prediction. Let us pursue the branch which follows from a prediction of 1 tub. The decision maker now faces the choice of which level of production to select. He/she has the choice of 1, 2 or 3 tubs. This situation is essentially the same as the situation portrayed for the decision maker in Figure 7.1. But in that situation the decision maker had no forecasts. Now the decision maker has forecasts, and as a result the probabilities at the end of each branch have changed. In Figure 7.1 the probabilities were 0.1, 0.5 and 0.4. Now they are 8/17ths, 5/17ths and 4/17ths. Using these revised probabilities and the outcomes indicated at the end of each branch, the expected value for the production of 1, 2 and 3 tubs can be shown to be £20, £7 and £(63.6).

The calculations of these expected values are set out in detail in Table 7.4. Part (a) shows the expected value table for the production decision, given that a prediction of 1 tub has been received. The calculations show that the expected value is maximised by the production of 1 tub. In this case, the maximum expected value is £20. The remaining sections of Table 7.4 show similar calculations, but given the prediction of 2 tubs and 3 tubs respectively. In each of these cases, the revised probabilities are used to calculate the expected values.

Each of the three maximum expected values, £20, £37.7 and £41.6, calculated in Table 7.4 follows from a particular prediction and assumes a particular production decision. For example, the maximum expected value of £20 follows from a demand prediction of 1 tub and assumes the production of 1 tub. The branches of the decision tree which generate this maximum expected value, following the prediction of 1 tub, are shown on Figure 7.2. However, to simplify the presentation, the branches which follow from predictions of 2 and 3 tubs have been omitted. The maximum expected values which follow each of the three predictions are shown below the rectangular boxes in the middle of the decision tree. At the time the decision maker has to decide whether or not to acquire the information, he/she does not know what the prediction will be on any particular day. Thus, the expected value assuming the information is acquired can be calculated by taking

TABLE 7.4
Tabular Layout

(a) *Given* prediction of 1 tub

Expected value table (in £s)	Actual demand			Expected value	
	1 8/17	2 5/17	3 4/17		
Production 1	9.4	5.9	4.7	20.0	Max. EV
Production 2	(28.2)	11.8	9.4	(7.0)	
Production 3	(65.9)	(11.8)	14.1	(63.6)	

(b) *Given* prediction of 2 tubs

Expected value table (in £s)	Actual demand			Expected value	
	1 1/45	2 40/45 ·	3 4/45		
Production 1	0.4	17.8	1.8	20.0	
Production 2	(1.3)	35.5	3.5	37.7	Max. EV
Production 3	(3.1)	(35.5)	5.3	(33.3)	

(c) *Given* prediction of 3 tubs

Expected value table (in £s)	Actual demand			Expected value	
	1 1/38	2 5/38	3 32/38		
Production 1	0.5	2.6	16.9	20.0	
Production 2	(1.6)	5.3	33.7	37.4	
Production 3	(3.7)	(5.3)	50.6	41.6	Max. EV

the three maximum expected values and multiplying by the probabilities of each of the predictions, as follows:

EV(with imperfect information)
$$= £20(0.17)+£37.7(0.45) + £41.6(0.38) = £36.2 \qquad (7.2)$$

The value of the imperfect information is therefore £6.2, i.e., £36.2 – £30. As expected, the value of this imperfect information is less than the value of the perfect information, £16, calculated earlier.

7.5   Discussion

The reader may feel that the above illustration is highly contrived. It relates to a particular type of situation which may not be applicable to very many businesses. However, the approach adopted in the illustration can be generalised to deal with the value of information in much wider settings. It will be demonstrated in Chapter 8 that information economics is in fact a generalisation of the approach adopted in this illustration. In that case, however, decisions will be analysed in terms of expected utilities rather than in terms of expected values. The introduction of utility functions adds an additional dimension to the problem (namely, the decision maker's attitude to risk), but it does not change the basic method of valuing information.

It is important to emphasise that the value placed on information, both in the analysis described in this chapter and also in information economics, is specific to the decision being considered. For instance, in the above illustration, any changes in the original probabilities of demand, or in the variable cost or sales revenue figures could give rise to different values for the information. As will be seen later, this is the general conclusion reached by writers who have explored the information economics approach.

Furthermore, it is worth re-emphasising a point that was made earlier: namely, information only has value if it changes decisions. In the above illustration, given the imperfect information, it was optimal for the ice-cream manufacturer to produce the predicted number of tubs, whereas in the absence of the information it was optimal to always produce 2 tubs. However, it is not always optimal to produce at the predicted level. For instance, with a different combination of probabilities, revenues and costs, the optimal production might be 2 tubs, whatever the prediction. In such a case, the information will have no value, as 2 tubs would have been produced in the absence of the information.

Finally, some comments are needed about the role of information in the above analysis. If the decision maker chooses to acquire the information, it will have the effect of revising the probabilities which are used in the expected value calculations, as was seen in the decision tree illustrated in Figure 7.2. In that instance, the original or prior probabilities of 0.1, 0.5 and 0.4 were revised to reflect the new information. With a predicted demand of 1 tub, the revised or posterior probabilities were 8/17ths, 5/17ths and 4/17ths. Other revised probabilities were calculated for demand predictions of 2 and 3 tubs. As will be discussed in Chapter 8, if the decision maker can specify all aspects of the decision problem, the role of information is limited to this revision of probabilities. But there may be other roles for information, as will be discovered in Chapter 9.

Information Economics 8

Chapter 7 illustrated the value of information in the context of a particular decision. In this chapter the work of information economists will be used to provide a formal structure for the analysis of such a problem. Information economics was developed in the late 1960s and early 1970s, notably by Marschak and Radner (1972). This work was firmly grounded in the statistical decision theory which was being used by accounting researchers to introduce uncertainty into their decision models; for instance, into C–V–P analysis and the variance investigation models discussed in Chapters 4 and 5.

The application of information economics to management accounting involves modelling mathematically decisions concerning the selection of accounting systems. In such problems a decision maker (or information evaluator) is confronted with a selection of accounting systems, each subject to uncertain costs and benefits. A description of an information economic model can be provided by generalising the illustration of the value of imperfect information described in Chapter 7.

8.1 The Ice-cream Manufacturer's Problem

Essentially, it may be recalled that the ice-cream manufacturer faced the problem of whether or not to acquire information concerning likely weather conditions. The analysis involved two steps. First, the decision maker's problem was analysed on the assumption that he/she did not acquire this information and second, the problem was analysed on the assumption that he/she did acquire the information. In the no information case the expected value for each action available to the decision maker was calculated, namely, the production of 1, 2 or 3 tubs of ice-cream. The action which led to the highest expected value was then selected. This maximum expected value reflected the average outcome if the decision maker did not acquire the information.

When the information was brought into the analysis it was necessary to calculate expected values for each possible signal, i.e., for demand predictions of 1, 2 or 3 tubs. For each possible signal, the expected value of each available action was calculated and the optimal action (the action which maximised expected value) was selected. This provided an optimal action and an associated expected value for each and every possible signal. Finally, the expected value of the decision situation with the information was computed using these optimal actions and the probabilities of each signal.

This method of analysis can be expressed mathematically using a modified information economics approach. The symbols which will be used are consistent with those adopted by Demski (1980). The decision maker faces the problem of selecting a particular action from a complete listing of all the actions available to him. Thus, if the letter a is used to refer to any specific action (or decision), then a belongs to the set of all possible actions, A. This is normally written as follows: $a \in A$. The ice-cream manufacturer had three possible actions – the production of 1, 2 or 3 tubs.

The outcome of each action is uncertain, as it is contingent upon a 'state of the world' existing after the action is taken. It is assumed that the decision maker can quantify the likely states of the world and their probabilities of occurrence. If s is used to represent any specific state of the world, we can write $s \in S$, where S represents the set of all possible states. In the ice-cream manufacturer's problem there were three possible states; namely, the three possible levels of demand – 1, 2 or 3 tubs. The probability of each state occurring can be expressed by a probability function, normally written as $\phi(s)$.

Now, any outcome will be the result of a combination of a particular action and a specific state of the world. This can be demonstrated by referring to the pay-off tables set out in the illustrations in Chapter 7, for example Table 7.2. Each element of a pay-off table reflects a particular combination of action and state. Thus, a particular outcome could be written as $f(a, s)$. The measurement basis for the outcome implied by this expression depends entirely on the problem at hand. For instance, in the ice-cream manufacturer's problem, the possible outcomes were measured in terms of the daily contribution earned on sales of ice-cream. In other problems, it might be appropriate to measure outcomes in terms of the net present value of future cash flows.

In the ice-cream manufacturer's problem the expected value of each action was calculated by multiplying the outcome for each state (given that action) by the probability of the state occurring. Mathematically this can be expressed, using the terms defined above, as follows:

$$EV(a) = \sum_{s \in S} f(a, s)\, \phi(s) \tag{8.1}$$

This is equivalent to summing across the rows of the expected value table (Table 7.2).

The decision maker's problem which, in this case, is stated in terms of selecting the action which maximises the expected value, can now be expressed as:

$$EV(a^*) = \max_{a \in A} EV(a)$$

$$= \max_{a \in A} \sum_{s \in S} f(a, s)\, \phi(s) \tag{8.2}$$

where a^* indicates the optimal action. In Table 7.2 this involved selecting the row (that is, the action) with the largest amount in the expected value column.

The above expressions are based on the assumption that the decision maker's objective is to maximise expected value. Information economics, however, is normally based on the assumption that the decision maker is a subjective expected utility maximiser. Adopting the objective of utility maximisation has enabled researchers to generalise the model to include a recognition of the decision maker's attitude to risk. The particular form of the utility function, which relates money values to the decision maker's subjective utility, will reflect the decision maker's preference for or aversion to risk. For purposes of the present analysis a completely general utility function will be assumed. In other words, the decision maker's assessment of the utility associated with any outcome will be expressed simply as $U(a, s)$. This expression could be evaluated mathematically provided the precise form of the decision maker's utility function can be established. But this is unnecessary for purposes of the present analysis.

The equations set out above defining the expected value from a particular action and the decision maker's objective can be restated in terms of expected utilities. The expected utility following from a particular action can be written as:

$$E(U|\text{a}) = \sum_{s \in S} U(a, s)\, \phi(s) \qquad (8.3)$$

where $E(U|\text{a})$ is the expected utility given that action a is undertaken. The decision maker's objective can be expressed in terms of selecting the action, a^*, which maximises expected utility, as follows:

$$E(U|\text{a}^*) = \max_{a \in A} E(U|a) \qquad (8.4)$$

This decision model relies on the assumption that the decision maker can quantify the following parameters:

A − the set of all possible actions available to the decision maker,
S − the set of all possible states of the world,
ϕ − the probability function expressed for all possible states of the world, and
U − the decision maker's utility function.

Each of these parameters will be dependent upon the decision maker's 'experience'. The model is said to be complete if all the parameters are correctly specified, in so far as they are perceived by the decision maker.

Equations (8.3) and (8.4) do not include an explicit recognition of information. However, the decision maker's experience, which determines the parameters of those equations, represents the sum total of the information he/she has received to date. In the context of information economics, the evaluation of information concerns the possibilities for acquiring additional information which would supplement the decision maker's experience. As was seen in the illustration discussed in Chapter 7, the only role for information in such models is to revise probabilities, i.e., to change the probability function expressing the likelihood of particular states of the world occurring. This will be demonstrated below.

8.2   The Role of Information

Suppose that there is an information system which would provide the decision maker, before he/she selects his/her action, with information concerning the likely future state of the world. The receipt of a message from this information system might cause him/her to revise his/her expectations concerning the state of the world and this, in turn, might influence the action which is selected. Consider a decision problem after the receipt of information – in information economics terms, assume that a signal, y, has been received from information system, η. In the ice-cream manufacturer's problem it was demonstrated that after the forecast had been received and a prediction made as to the likely demand, the decision problem became one of selecting the optimum action given the revised probabilities. The expected utility from a given action can now be expressed as follows:

$$E(U|a, y, \eta) = \sum_{s \in S} U(a, s, \eta) \, \phi(s|y, \eta) \qquad (8.5)$$

and the decision maker's objective as:

$$E(U|y, \eta) = \max_{a \in A} E(U|a, y, \eta) \qquad (8.6)$$

The term $E(U|y, \eta)$ represents the expected utility which will follow from the receipt of signal, y, from information system, η. This expected utility arises from selecting the action which maximises the expected utility given the signal, y, from the information system, η, i.e., $E(U|a, y, \eta)$. In evaluating the utility from each outcome the term, η, is added to the state-action combination, giving the expression $U(a,s,\eta)$. This additional term is included in the expression to indicate that there will be some cost of using the information system. Finally, it should be noted that in equation (8.5) the revised probabilities, $\phi(s|y,\eta)$, are used in place of the simple expression of probabilities, $\phi(s)$, which appeared in equation (8.3). The revised probabilities reflect the new information that has been provided by the signal, y, from information system, η.

In the ice-cream manufacturer's problem the probabilities of the three states of the world were originally 0.1, 0.5 and 0.4. Following the weather forecast, and the associated predictions of demand, revised probabilities were used. In the case of a predicted demand of 1 tub, the revised probabilities were 8/17ths, 5/17ths and 4/17ths. These revised probabilities are equivalent to $\phi(s|y, \eta)$, whereas the original probabilities are equivalent to $\phi(s)$. As indicated in Chapter 7 the revised probabilities can be computed directly using Bayes' theorem.

8.3 Bayes' Theorem

Bayes' theorem is used to revise probabilities for new information. It was used in Chapter 6 to revise probabilities to reflect the new information provided by variance analysis. The derivation of the theorem is explained in most statistical textbooks. Its general form can be written as follows:

$$P(A|B) = \frac{\Pr(B|A)\Pr(A)}{\Pr(B)} \tag{8.7}$$

In terms of the ice-cream manufacturer's problem, A would represent the actual demand and B the predicted demand. Thus, consider the probability of 1 tub actually being demanded following the prediction of 1 tub. Revised probabilities can be calculated using Bayes' theorem, as follows:

Pr (Demand 1|Prediction 1)

$$= \frac{\text{Pr(Prediction 1|Demand 1)Pr(Demand 1)}}{\text{Pr(Prediction 1)}} \qquad (8.8)$$

Consider each of the terms on the right-hand side. The probability of a prediction of 1 tub, given an actual demand of 1 tub, is 0.8, i.e., the reliability of the forecast. The probability of a demand of 1 tub is the prior probability of 0.1. The denominator requires a further calculation, however.

The probability of predicting 1 tub has to be considered in three parts. There is the probability that 1 tub will be predicted when the demand is actually 1 tub and also there is the probability of 1 tub being predicted when the demand is in fact either 2 or 3 tubs. The probability of an actual demand of 1 tub together with the prediction of 1 tub is 0.1 (the probability of the actual demand) multiplied by 0.8 (the probability of the prediction), i.e., $(0.1)(0.8)=0.08$. The probability of the prediction of 1 tub with an actual demand of 2 tubs is 0.5 (the probability of the actual demand of 2 tubs) multiplied by 0.1 (the probability of a prediction of 1 tub when the demand is actually 2 tubs), i.e., $(0.5)(0.1)=0.05$. Similarly, the probability of a prediction of 1 with an actual demand of 3 tubs will be $(0.4)(0.1)=0.04$. Thus,

Pr(Prediction 1)
$$= (0.1)(0.8)+(0.5)(0.1)+(0.4)(0.1) = 0.17 \qquad (8.9)$$

Now the probability of 1 tub being demanded, given the prediction of 1 tub, can be calculated using equation (8.8):

$$\text{Pr(Demand 1|Prediction 1)} = \frac{(0.8)(0.1)}{(0.17)} = \frac{0.08}{0.17}$$

$$= 8/17 \qquad (8.10)$$

This is the same probability as calculated in Table 7.3. The probabilities of the other levels of demand, following the prediction of 1 tub, can be calculated in a similar manner; as also can the probabilities for the different levels of demand given the other two possible signals. The reader might like to check that the use of Bayes' theorem, as set out above, gives the same answer in each case as the calculations in Table 7.3.

8.4 Value of Information

Once the expected utility of the optimal action given each possible signal from the information system, $E(U|y, \eta)$ for $y \in Y$, has been calculated, the expected utility of the decision situation with the information system can be determined. Formally, this can be expressed as:

$$E(U|\eta) = \sum_{y \in Y} (U|y, \eta) \, \phi(y|\eta) \tag{8.11}$$

In this calculation the expected utilities are summed across all possible signals, $y \in Y$. This is equivalent to the calculation which was performed in the ice-cream manufacturer's problem in order to compute the expected value with information of £36.2. Note that the probabilities used, $\phi(y|\eta)$, reflect the probability of each signal being produced by the information system. In the ice-cream manufacturer's problem these probabilities were 0.17, 0.45 and 0.38 – see Table 7.3 and Figure 7.2. The probability of 1 tub being signalled, 0.17, was calculated in equation (8.9). Similar calculations can be performed for the signals of 2 and 3 tubs, 0.45 and 0.38 respectively.

The term 'value of information' implies a monetary measure of value. This was easy to obtain when the analysis was expressed in terms of expected values. For instance, the value of the imperfect information to the ice-cream manufacturer was £6.2, which was calculated by taking the expected value with the imperfect information, £36.2, and deducting the expected value without the information, £30. The measurement of value becomes difficult, however, when the analysis is expressed in terms of expected utilities.

At the simplest level, it can be said that one information system, η_1, is at least as good as another, η_2, if and only if

$$E(U|\eta_1) \geq E(U|\eta_2) \tag{8.12}$$

i.e., the expected utility of the decision situation with the first information system is at least as great as the expected utility with the second information system. Unfortunately, the difference between two expected utility measures cannot be easily converted to a monetary value. As utility functions are normally non-linear, increments in utility cannot be evaluated in money terms independently of the absolute amounts of utility involved. Particular increments of utility will represent different amounts of monetary value at various points on the utility function. Thus, it is necessary to determine a monetary equivalent of the expected utility of each information system.

It may be possible to estimate a monetary value of an information system by eliciting from the decision maker the amount he/she would require in order to be persuaded to sell the decision opportunity (including the information system). For instance, if an amount k_1 is required in order to persuade the decision maker to part with the decision opportunity, including the information system, then it follows that:

$$U(k_1) = E(U|\eta_1) \tag{8.13}$$

Furthermore, if we can also identify that the decision maker would require an amount of k_0 to part with the decision opportunity, if the information system were not available, then it might be concluded that:

$$\text{Value of information} = k_1 - k_0 \tag{8.14}$$

8.5   The Selection of an Information System

The analysis outlined above recognised only two situations: the first was equated with no information (other than the information already impounded in the decision maker's experiences) and the second included one further information source. However, there may be a number of alternative information systems which are available to the decision maker. The selection of a preferred information system can be included in the analysis if it is assumed that the characteristics of all available information systems can be specified.

Each information system will provide a signal (from the set of all possible signals) which the decision maker can use to revise his/her expectations concerning the likely future states of the world. For completeness, the set of signals is taken to include 'no signal' and the set of information systems to include 'no system'. In order to analyse the selection of an information system it is necessary to identify all the decisions which might be taken by the decision maker following the receipt of each possible signal, from each possible information system. The result will be a series of equations in the form of equation (8.11); one equation for each available information system. The selection of a preferred system can then be expressed in terms of maximising the expected utility to be derived from using an information system. Formally this can be written as:

$$E(U|\eta^*) = \max_{\eta \in H} E(U|\eta) \tag{8.15}$$

where H represents the set of possible information systems.

The initial contributions to the information economics literature recognised only a single individual who selects both the information system and the action to be undertaken. However, later works gave some consideration to the possibility of task specialisation, i.e., the separation of the production and use of information. In such a case, the information system would be selected by an information evaluator and the action by a decision maker.

In general, the preferences in models with task specialisation are those of the information evaluator, who is sometimes regarded as the accountant. In selecting an information system the information evaluator must make predictions about the decision maker's responses to the signals that the information system will generate. As the outcomes in the model described above are dependent upon the actions taken by the decision maker, an information evaluator who wishes to maximise his/her expected utility must predict the actions which will be selected by the decision maker following each signal from each possible information system. The model, however, does not explicitly consider the motivations of the decision maker; for instance, what causes a decision maker to select a particular course of action when the outcome of that action accrues to the information evaluator or to the owner of the business. Such motivations require explicit consideration, but were beyond the scope of the information economics literature as it developed in the early 1970s. However, a particular extension of information economics, known as Agency Theory, does examine these problems. A consideration of Agency Theory is deferred until Chapter 10.

8.6 Discussion

The primary focus of information economics in the management accounting literature was on the information system choice problem outlined above. It should be remembered that management accounting (and accounting in general) is concerned with information systems. A particular contribution of the information economics approach was the clarification of the role of management accounting research. Demski suggested three ways in which the researcher can assist the practising management accountant in his role as an information evaluator:

(1) The analysis of specific choice problems,
(2) The generation of new system alternatives, and
(3) The production of information for the policy maker (Demski, 1973, p. 74).

The analysis of specific choice problems represents an extension of the decision models described in Chapters 4, 5 and 6. The information economics approach, however, emphasised the importance of considering the role of information within these models. The generation of new system alternatives will assist 'the information evaluator to make a more complete listing of possible information systems. Techniques, such as linear programming, multiple regression and opportunity costing might not be considered by individual management accountants/information evaluators in practice unless they are brought to their attention by researchers. However, the generation of new alternatives must be distinguished from their tests in actual applications. This is the third role for the management accounting researcher. The testing of system alternatives, either empirically or analytically, will provide the information evaluator with information about the costs and difficulties of implementing particular alternatives. This third role for management accounting research includes the evaluation of alternative accounting methods and the comparison of simple and complex models. Such evaluations and comparisons were pursued in the accounting literature as a result of developments in the area of information economics – see discussion in Chapter 9.

The information economics model described in this chapter is a normative model, in that it purports to show how information systems 'ought' to be selected. However, even its main proponents admitted that there are too many variables to be identified and its complexity is more than can be handled. This admission led some writers to dismiss the approach. Nevertheless some useful contributions were made by researchers who explored the implications of information economics for the study of management accounting. At this point it is worth briefly summarising some of these contributions. But, as will be described in Chapters 9 and 10, additional models are needed to analyse the role of information in management accounting practice.

The information system choice problem described above requires a complete specification of the information evaluator's decision problem. A complete analysis is unlikely to be practicable for various reasons. It may be too expensive, or individuals may be incapable of identifying the available alternatives and/or completely specifying their preferences. In such cases, a modified or simplified analysis may be undertaken. The analysis of simplified models, which is discussed in Chapter 9, has provided a basis for understanding the roles of the simple models that are frequently observed in practice. Such models may actually be 'optimal' when information costs and specification issues are considered. The specification of the complete model is necessary, however, in order to provide the theoretical basis for an analysis of simplified models. As will be seen in Chapter 9, information has an important role to play in simplified models.

In the complete analysis, described in this chapter, the role of information is limited to the systematic revision of expectations concerning future states. Although this level of analysis was able to clarify the role of information, it did not yield any general implications concerning the production of information – in other words, concerning the management accounting techniques which should be used. Demski and Feltham reached the conclusion that 'whether one cost assessment alternative is preferred to another is an inherently contextual question' (1976, p. 249). Such a conclusion means that appropriate accounting techniques can be determined only in the context of the decision situation and in particular, by reference to the specific costs and benefits of the information for that decision. This is the 'costly truth' approach.

'Costly truth' implies that although truth can be attained (i.e., a preferred accounting system can be identified) it will vary from one situation to another according to the costs and benefits of information. Truth, in this sense, is the normatively determined accounting system – the system that ought to be used, given all the relevant costs and benefits. Viewed in this way, the information economics approach is not fundamentally different from the economic framework which underlies management accounting's conventional wisdom – as described in Chapter 2. But now, uncertainty and information costs are explicitly recognised in the analysis. The information economics approach, however, separates the choice made by the decision maker from the choice made by the information evaluator.

An important contribution of information economics to management accounting research was that it encouraged researchers to identify separately information system choice and information system design. Previously researchers had focused exclusively on the design issues and this had resulted in a succession of new and increasingly complex techniques as already described. In general, textbooks which contain discussions of management accounting under conditions of uncertainty usually focus only on the design issues. There is little explicit discussion of the information costs and benefits associated with individual techniques. However, an awareness of the information system choice problem led some researchers to explore the costs and benefits of applying certain management accounting techniques in practice and, especially, to examine the relative advantages of simple and complex models. The results of their research will be discussed in the next chapter.

Simplified Models and Empirical Studies 9

The practical usefulness of the complex models developed in areas such as C–V–P analysis and variance investigations (discussed in Chapters 4 and 5) can be questioned because of the difficulties and costs associated with their implementation. For instance, the necessary information may not be available within the constraints imposed by current information technology and the ability of existing management. Furthermore, even if such information could be provided, the costs of so doing may be extremely high. It has been argued in previous chapters that, in general, the costs of providing information should not outweigh the benefits to be obtained therefrom.

Simple, and sometimes apparently 'unrealistic', techniques are frequently observed in practice, despite an extensive literature which provides complex, and 'more realistic', alternatives. The insights into the costs and benefits of accounting systems gained from a study of information economics can provide a basis for comparing simple and complex management accounting models and techniques. However, the form of the information system choice problem which was described in Chapter 8 is not suitable for the purpose of exploring the use of simple models and 'rule-of-thumb' techniques. In this chapter an information economics analysis of simplified models will be described and its implications for empirical studies of management accounting will be discussed.

9.1   Revisions to the 'Complete' Analysis

The analysis of information system choice described in Chapter 8 requires a complete specification of the information evaluator's decision problem. Such a complete analysis may be impracticable for various reasons. It may be too expensive to implement, or individuals may be incapable of identifying all the available alternatives and/or completely specifying their preferences. It is generally recognised, even by the advocates of the information economics approach, that the complete model is unlikely to be useful to the practitioner. It is far too complex and far too costly. Accordingly, a modified or simplified analysis is needed.

In information economics terms, *modification* occurs when the complete analysis is altered, but identification of the preferred action is nevertheless guaranteed, while *simplification* occurs when alteration of the complete analysis cannot guarantee identification of the preferred action. For this purpose the preferred action is the one which would be selected if the decision problem could be completely specified. As the preferred course of action is not guaranteed by a simplified model, the use of such a model may involve a loss, or a cost which arises from the difference between the expected utility of the decision situation with the simplified model and the maximum expected utility of that decision situation with a complete analysis. In practice, however, it may be very difficult to measure this cost, because of the problems of specifying the complete model – as will be discussed below.

The analysis of departures from the complete model provide a basis for understanding the role of the simple models that are frequently observed in practice. Such simple models might actually be 'optimal', when information costs and specification issues are considered. Although the actions selected using a simplified model may differ from the actions which would have been selected by a complete analysis, the apparent losses incurred through use of simple models may be less than the information costs associated with the complete analysis. Demski and Feltham (1976, p. 58) characterised their study of simplified decision models as an attempt to balance, in an economic manner, the costs of analysis against the possibility of inferior analysis and choice.

In the complete analysis, the role of information is limited to the systematic revision of expectations (or probabilities) concerning future states. When simplified decision models are used information may also indicate a need for the models themselves to be revised. For example, after particular decisions have been taken information may become available which indicates that the choices made could have been improved in some way. Such 'feedback' information about the outcome of past choices can be particularly important as it may provide a basis for adapting or evolving the decision model, as well as altering current decisions.

As already pointed out, when simplified models are used decisions may differ from the preferred courses of action which would have followed from a complete analysis. If in practice the complete analysis is infeasible, however, there will be no way of measuring the loss incurred through model simplification. (But it seems reasonable to suggest that the simpler the model, the greater the potential loss.) In such situations, it is essential to monitor the outcomes of past choices, with a view to improving current or future decisions. This monitoring process may suggest possibilities for improving decision making by revising the simplified model currently in use – either by making further simplifications or by adding 'complexities'. The expected benefits of such changes should be assessed against the likely change in information costs. Thus, although it will generally be infeasible to evaluate the absolute loss through model simplification, it may nevertheless be possible to estimate the likely benefits of revisions to an existing simplified model.

It should be noted that the so-called 'complete analysis' is in fact only a partial analysis of the information costs involved. The costs of undertaking the complete analysis are not considered in the model. The costs of specifying all the alternative courses of action, states of the world, etc., are ignored. Nevertheless, the complete analysis provides a valuable benchmark for understanding the problems involved in selecting accounting information systems. In the following sections of this chapter some aspects of model simplification will be described and illustrated. The implications of such simplification are discussed towards the end of the chapter.

9.2   Form of Model Simplification

The complete analysis described in Chapter 8 contained the following decision model, which assumes that the decision maker has received a particular signal from his/her information system (see equations (8.5) and (8.6)):

$$E(U|y, \eta) = \max_{a \in A} \sum_{s \in S} U(a, s, \eta)\, \phi(s|y, \eta) \qquad (9.1)$$

The decision model requires the decision maker to specify the following:

A – the complete set of available actions,
S – the complete set of state variables,
$U(\cdot)$ – the form of the utility function, and
$\phi(\cdot)$ – the form of the probability function for state variables.

Demski (1980) suggests simplifying each of the above elements of the decision model. For instance, a restricted set of available actions and a restricted set of states of the world could be used together with a simple probability function and a simple utility function.

The set of available actions could be simplified by restricting attention to some particular subset. For instance, attention could be restricted to particular 'decision variables', while all other variables are assumed to remain unchanged. Consider a decision concerning the production plan for a coming period. The decision maker might consider the level of output for each of a restricted number of products (the decision variables). He/she would then disregard the possibility of producing other products, and in addition assume that other variables, such as available capacity, efficiency, etc., remain constant. The specification may be further simplified by considering only a particular range for each of the decision variables – that is, production of the various products within a 'relevant range'. The notion of a relevant range is quite common in most management accounting textbooks.

The specification of state variables can be simplified by restricting attention to a particular subset of the possible states. This subset could contain only the more likely states – the more unlikely states being omitted from consideration. It could be further assumed that a single state variable could capture the essence of a number of possible state variables. For instance, the sales demand for a company's products might be characterised as high, medium, or low, in which case only these three possible states of the world would be considered. A state variable such as sales demand implies a number of underlying states: the state of the economy, government policy, relative prices, general inflation, etc. At the extreme, the state specification could be restricted to a single value on one state variable – in other words, certainty could be assumed.

The simplification of the probability function will, to a large extent, follow the simplification of the state specification. If a restricted number of states are considered, the probability function need only encompass those states. In addition, the form of the probability distribution might be simplified, for instance, by using a normal distribution or some other standard distribution.

Finally, the specification of the decision maker's utility function can also be simplified. For instance, maximising expected values could be used as the basis for decision making. This form of analysis was used in Chapter 7. In fact, it could be argued that the model described in Chapter 7 was actually a simplified model. Only a restricted set of actions and states of the world were considered and the decision maker's objective was assumed to be expected value maximisation. A further illustration of a simplified model is set out below.

9.3 Illustration

Given the various types of model simplification described above, it would appear that linear programming provides a good example of a simplified decision model. As an illustration, consider a linear programming problem in which the production and sale of three products, X, Y and Z, with respective contributions of £10, £12 and £15, are evaluated in the context of constraints on the available labour and machine hours. With appropriate assumptions about the amount of labour and machine hours required to produce each of the products, the following linear programming problem could be formulated:

$$\max 10X + 12Y + 15Z$$
$$X + Y + Z \geq 40\,000 \text{ (labour hours)}$$
$$2X + 3Y + 4Z \geq 100\,000 \text{ (machine hours)}$$

This model involves several simplifications. The actions contemplated by the decision maker are restricted to the production and sale of the three decision variables, products X, Y and Z. The productive capacity is assumed to be limited to 40 000 labour hours and 100 000 machine hours. The possibilities for increasing this capacity are not included in the model. Furthermore, the analysis is limited to linear functions, which imply that the prices of three products are fixed, that the costs of production can be analysed into fixed and variable elements, that the productive resources are divisible, etc.

Only one state of the world was considered. It is assumed that all the parameters of the model are known with certainty. (The analysis could be extended, however, by considering alternative formulations of the linear programme using different values for individual parameters.) As a result of the state simplification the probability function implied in the model is very simple – the assumed probability is 1.0 for all the parameters. Finally, it is assumed that the utility to the decision maker can be represented in terms of the contribution earned by each of the three products.

This formulation of the decision problem could be made more complex, for instance by considering the production of certain products for stock, or the sale of existing stocks. Alternatively, the formulation could be further simplified, for instance by ignoring the relative scarcity of productive resources and simply producing the product which earns the highest contribution per unit. The decision maker must choose the form of the model to be used. In general terms, the simpler the model, the greater the risk that the resulting decision will not be the optimal, in the sense that it will not be the decision which would have been made if a complete analysis were available. But there will be additional costs associated with using the more complex models. The decision maker must attempt to balance these additional costs against the possibility of taking sub-optimal decisions.

As discussed earlier, in practice it may be impossible to quantify the *absolute* costs of failing to take the decisions which are optimal in the above sense. Nevertheless, model choice can still be evaluated in terms of costs and benefits, as it should be possible to compare the *relative* costs and benefits of alternative simplified models. For example, simulation and/or sensitivity analysis could be used to estimate the likely benefits of the various available models. Furthermore, feedback information may help in the assessment of the reliability of these estimates and in the identification of needs and opportunities for model revision.

The above discussion demonstrates that the choice of a particular form of simplified decision model requires a decision to be taken by the decision maker. Thus, the decision maker is faced with two separate but related decisions. First, a decision model has to be selected and second, a course of action has to be chosen using the selected decision model. However, the choice of action indicated by the decision model must be used with caution. A simplified decision model can provide information to the decision maker, but it does not represent a complete analysis of the decision problem. There may be other factors which the decision maker will wish to weigh in his/her ultimate selection of a course of action to be followed. For instance, in deciding how much to produce of the three products, X, Y and Z, the decision maker may want to consider the effect on goodwill of a decision to drop one or more of the products.

In describing the complete model in Chapter 8 it was pointed out that the role of information in that model is restricted to the revision of probabilities concerning future states of the world. In the simplified analysis, however, feedback information can lead to changes in the decision model. Feedback information, such as the outcome of a particular period's production and sales might indicate that the contributions on products Y and Z are rather less than anticipated and that another product is available, say product W. The parameters of the linear programming might then be altered to incorporate the additional product and the revised contributions might be used in the objective functions. Furthermore the decision maker might revise the decision model to allow for the possibility of expanding capacity in order to produce the additional product.

In reaching any decision concerning an expansion of capacity the decision maker would probably consider courses of action which were omitted from the simplified decision model – for example, purchasing new machines, introducing shift work, etc. The outcome of such a capacity decision might then prompt a revision of the operating decision model which had been used previously. In the above illustration the linear programming decision maker could use and thus model choice is a decision revised action set. But in other cases, the information might cause the decision model to be further simplified.

In general terms, feedback information provides the decision maker with a means of monitoring and, where necessary, revising decision models. There is no such role for information in the complete analysis.

To summarise, the above discussion highlights three points of interest. First, there are many alternative simplifications which the decision maker could use and thus, model choice is a decision which can be analysed in terms of costs and benefits. Second, the decision maker does not necessarily delegate the decision to the model, rather the model provides additional information which will be used in the decision maker's further evaluations. Third, information has an expanded role in the simplified analysis – it can lead to revisions of the decision model.

9.4   Implications for Empirical Work

It was suggested in earlier chapters, particularly in the chapters dealing with C–V–P analysis and variance investigation models, that management accounting researchers in the late 1960s and early 1970s were attempting to develop ideal (or 'realistic') models. Attempts were made to relax assumptions which were included, either implicitly or explicitly, in the simpler models developed somewhat earlier in the 1960s. However, now that the nature of information economics and, in particular, the role of simplified analysis have been examined it should be clear that it will not necessarily be 'optimal' for decision makers to opt for the apparently more realistic models.

In the earlier discussion, the term 'optimal decision' referred to the selection of the preferred action according to the complete model described in Chapter 8. But in terms of the simplified analysis, optimality has to reflect a balancing of the relative costs and benefits of the available models. The choice of a particular model will depend on the costs and benefits of that model, relative to the costs and benefits of alternative models. It would be quite reasonable ('optimal') for a decision maker to select a very simple model, if the costs of using the more complex alternatives exceed their benefits.

Some researchers have attempted to examine empirically the relationship between simple and complex models. The examination of alternative variance investigation models undertaken by Magee (1976) will be used as a first illustration.

Magee was concerned to identify reasons for the limited use, in practice, of the various models for variance investigation which had been proposed in the academic literature – some of these models were discussed in Chapter 6. He began his paper by a reference to the information economics literature, in particular the work of Demski and Feltham (1976), and proceeded to construct an information system choice framework which described the decision maker's model selection problem. This framework adopted the model simplification approach described above.

The choice facing the decision maker in Magee's framework is the selection of a decision model. No action variables were included, as it was assumed that the selection of a decision model would imply a particular action for each and every signal that the model generates. In simple terms, it was assumed that if the decision model indicates that an investigation should take place, then an investigation will follow. In this way, the decision maker's actions are entailed in the selection of the decision model.

Ideally, the maximisation of expected utility should be the criterion for selecting a decision model. Each decision model implies a particular set of actions which could, in theory, be evaluated in terms of expected utility. However, because of the difficulties of measuring utility, Magee evaluated variance investigation models by reference to a decision maker's pay-off function expressed in terms of the expected costs and benefits of the investigation process. This led Magee to a model choice framework which was operationalised as an 'expected annual cost minimisation' problem. The costs of using the available variance investigation models were evaluated and then compared to the relative benefits derived from each model. Simulation was used as a means of measuring both the costs and benefits of investigation.

Seven variance investigation models were included in the study. These models reflected increasing amounts of complexity. Model 1 involved investigating all unfavourable cost variances, while 2, 3 and 4 involved investigations if the actual costs exceeded the standard by at least 10 per cent, one standard deviation and two standard deviations, respectively. The decision theory model of Dyckman (1969) and the dynamic programming model of Kaplan (1969) were used as the basis of models 5 and 6. Finally to provide a benchmark, model 7 was based on a dynamic programming approach assuming perfect information.

The simulation analysis suggested that increasing the complexity of variance investigation models yields little or no benefit in a cost minimisation sense, when both operating costs and investigation costs are recognised. Furthermore, if a manager is assessed only in terms of operating costs he/she would be acting quite rationally by investigating all unfavourable cost variances (model 1). Magee concluded that there was 'no overwhelming evidence that a manager who uses a "naive model" is making a poor model choice decision. In fact, the opposite may be true' (1976, pp. 542–3). The added costs of estimating parameters and solving the decision problem may outweigh the potential benefits to be derived from a complex model. However, the information and implementation costs will vary with the situation, likewise the potential benefits. Thus, the model choice decision is situation specific. This conclusion agrees with the general findings of the information economics approach which was described in Chapter 8.

Magee's analysis also demonstrated that the method of assessing managerial performance can affect model choice. For instance, a manager who is assessed only in terms of his department's operating costs (no recognition being made of investigation costs) is likely to be motivated to select the model which investigates all unfavourable variances. Such behavioural effects were not explicitly considered in the early information economics research, but they are recognised in the agency theory models which are discussed in Chapter 10. The information economics approach described in this and the preceding two chapters, with its emphasis on information costs and benefits, may help explain certain aspects of current practice, but other (behavioural) factors may also be important and need incorporating in the models.

A subsequent study examined cost variance investigation models in an empirical setting (Jacobs, 1978). That study also failed to identify a single superior model, although it was possible to conclude that certain models are better than other models in particular circumstances. But Jacobs was wisely cautious in not attempting to generalise his findings.

Although capital investment decisions are not explicitly reviewed in this book, it is worth noting that a similar comparison of simple and complex models was attempted in that area. Sundem (1974) performed a simulation study of capital investment decisions which has many parallels with Magee's work on variance investigation models. The application of information economics to accounting also provided the stimulus for Sundem's analysis, and his simulations led to the identical conclusion that model choice is situation specific.

Both Magee and Sundem used simulation to study the cost effectiveness of simple and complex models. An earlier study by Klammer had attempted to identify whether the cost effectiveness of alternative decision models can be observed in operating performance (1973). Klammer's null hypothesis was that the use of complex (sophisticated) techniques for capital investment appraisal is not associated with superior performance. This hypothesis could not be rejected by the study. Klammer concluded that 'the mere adoption of various analytical tools is not sufficient to bring about superior performance' (1973, p. 361).

The above studies emphasise the important conclusion that the use in practice of simple techniques and rules-of-thumb can, in certain circumstances, represent optimal responses to the cost and benefits of information provision. This conclusion, which is consistent with the results of analysis by information economics researchers, does not mean that complex models should be ignored. Such models should be developed and, where appropriate, made available to information evaluators in practice who can then make model choices on a cost/benefit basis. But the quest for complexity in decision models, simply as a means of better representing the underlying reality, is not necessarily going to provide 'ideal models' which will be more useful to practitioners than the rather simpler models already available. The choice of any particular model, simple or complex, will depend on the estimated costs and benefits of that model, relative to the estimated costs and benefits of alternative models.

9.5 A Change of Emphasis

As described in earlier chapters, management accounting research in the early 1970s attempted to refine the economic framework which forms the basis of management accounting's conventional wisdom. By the middle of the decade two particular refinements, uncertainty and information costs, had been explored. The combined effects of these refinements led researchers to question the prescriptive power of that conventional wisdom. In particular, are the techniques derived through a 'conditional truth' approach generally applicable in a world of uncertainty and information costs?

The work of the information economics researchers indicated that no general prescriptions can be made. This conclusion suggests that the conventional wisdom of management accounting does not necessarily provide the basis for best practice, although it may provide techniques which can be useful in certain circumstances. Furthermore, the studies which demonstrated that simple or rule-of-thumb techniques may be the 'optimal' reaction to the costs and benefits of information provision meant that practitioners should not necessarily be criticised for failing to implement the conventional wisdom.

An apparent consequence of the studies of simple and complex models was that subsequent research became much more concerned with explaining the reasons for particular practices, than with making normative statements. In this context, normative statements indicate the actions which ought to be taken in practice (e.g., the accounting practices which ought to be used by practictioners) based on some assumed business objectives. The search for explanations of observed practices may be termed an explanatory theory approach. An explanatory theory in the present context is a theory which provides an explanation for the use of particular accounting practices.

An example may help to illustrate the change of emphasis in management accounting research. In 1938 Baxter observed that the allocation of overheads in practice may provide an approximate allowance for opportunity cost; but he argued that accountants should not rely on this approximation (1938, p. 273). He and his colleagues at the London School of Economics suggested that the measurement of opportunity costs could improve accounting practice. Their work on the role of opportunity costs in accounting provided an important conceptual base for the decision user (or conditional truth) approach, which is fundamental to management accounting's conventional wisdom.

In 1979 Zimmerman made a similar observation, but without reference to Baxter's earlier paper. Zimmerman, however, attempted to explain the use of such approximations as a rational choice within an agency theory framework. He argued that if overheads are frequently allocated in practice 'it is likely that the technique is yielding benefits that exceed its costs' (1979, p. 519). For instance, the perceived costs of obtaining more accurate measurements of the 'difficult to observe' opportunity costs probably exceed the losses caused by using overhead allocations as approximation. Zimmerman's discussion of cost allocations will be considered further in Chapter 10. For the present, it is sufficient to note that the approaches of Baxter and Zimmerman were quite different. Whereas Baxter's concern was to provide prescriptions for practice, Zimmerman's aim was to explain practice.

Other researchers using, for instance, agency theory models (which are described in Chapter 10) have attempted to demonstrate that conditions exist in which the management accounting techniques observed in practice can be shown to be the outcome of rational choice. Although such models may be a long way from providing a complete explanatory theory of management accounting practice, they do offer some insights.

The search for such explanation reflects a fundamental change in management accounting research. Faced with the gap between theory and practice the conventional approach was to suggest that it takes time for new techniques to be learned and then implemented by practitioners – but given sufficient time and a widespread education programme the techniques will eventually be used in practice. Following the change of emphasis in management accounting research in the 1970s, current researchers faced with the same gap have attempted to modify their theories to encompass and explain existing practice. The test of good theory in management accounting has come to include its power in explaining existing practice. For instance, in reviewing agency theory as a framework for management accounting, Baiman (1982) suggested that one test of a theory's usefulness and an indication of the extent to which confidence can be placed in its implications is whether its explanation of the use of accounting information coincides with the uses observed in practice.

The change of emphasis during the 1970s has, to some extent, brought closer together the quantitative and behavioural approaches to research in management accounting. At the beginning of the decade behavioural research was almost totally separate from research in the quantitative areas of management accounting. But by the end of the decade both behavioural researchers and their more quantitatively inclined colleagues were looking for theories to explain observed management accounting practice.

9.6   Some Comments on Behavioural Accounting Research

Although a detailed discussion of behavioural accounting is outside the scope of this book, some comments will be useful in order to put developments in quantitative management accounting research into perspective. Interest in behavioural accounting research developed rapidly in the 1960s alongside, but quite separate from, the development of management accounting's conventional wisdom. Although much of this behavioural research was fragmentary, several major strands followed from the recognition that existing management accounting practices could have dysfunctional consequences. In particular, attention was given to the behavioural effects of budgets and to the influence of accounting information on decision-making behaviour.

Behavioural accounting researchers have given most attention over the years to research on individual (or human) information processing and decision making. It is only relatively recently that research in organisational behaviour has had a significant influence on behavioural accounting. This latter development coincided with pleas for relevance in behavioural research in accounting. This is not to imply that the many papers on human information processing in accounting are irrelevant, but to date few of these studies have examined individuals in organisational settings.

The pioneers in behavioural accounting research, stimulated by particular accounting problems, were aware of the need for relevance in their studies. But frequently relevance (or external validity) was achieved only at the expense of internal validity, i.e., the internal controls applied to the experimental situation. This exposed the researchers to criticism when their work was judged as experiments in behavioural science. Subsequently, behavioural accountants gave greater attention to the methodological sophistication of their laboratory experiments and the rigours of their hypothesis testing, but at the expense of the relevance (external validity) of their studies.

Several attempts were made during the 1960s and 1970s to introduce theories of organisational behaviour into management accounting. Probably the most well known organisational behaviour theory to appear in the management accounting literature is the behavioural theory of the firm developed by Cyert and March (1963). But in addition, the garbage can model of Cohen *et al.* (1972) and Cohen and March (1974), and Weick's organising model (1969 and 1979), amongst others, have been discussed in accounting contexts. Nevertheless, at the end of the 1970s Hopwood observed: 'it has to be admitted that as yet we have precious few descriptions, let alone understandings, of accounting systems as they operate in organisations' (1979, p. 145).

The organisation-based approach which had most impact on management accounting thought in the 1970s was contingency theory. The organisational contingency theorists argued that an appropriate model of organisation – in other words, its structure and management – depends on a number of factors. In general, these factors reflect aspects of the uncertainty faced by the organisation; for example, its technology and environment. The contingency theory approach to management accounting is based on the premise that there is no universally appropriate accounting system which applies equally to all organisations in all circumstances. A number of papers which attempted to develop this approach appeared in the management accounting literature. It was argued by the writers of such papers (sometimes implicitly) that contingent variables influence organisational design, which in turn influences the accounting system. Otley (1980) critically reviewed the contingency theory literature and concluded that although there might be a *prima facie* case for the development of a contingency framework for management accounting, care must be exercised in pursuing this line of research. In particular, management accounting systems should be studied in the widest possible organisational context.

The contingency theory approach, and indeed most of the organisation theory-based approaches, view the management accounting system as a means of achieving organisational control. The provision of information to facilitate decision making is an important element of the control process, but not the *raison d'être* for the system. In the description of management accounting's conventional wisdom in Chapter 2 the decision-making focus of management accounting was evident. Furthermore, both the conditional truth and the costly truth approaches are concerned with identifying information inputs for decision making processes – and control issues are discussed from within such a decision making perspective. However, organisation theory approaches tend to focus directly on control issues – and information for decision making follows from the specification of an appropriate control system. But, as will be demonstrated in Chapter 10, the control process is becoming an important focus for some of the more quantitatively inclined management accounting researchers who had previously concentrated on decision making processes.

Agency theory stresses the role of performance evaluation and motivation in achieving organisational objectives. This focus on a control process could be regarded as a further change of emphasis in management accounting research. Researchers are now giving particular attention to control processes and attempting to develop explanatory theories of management accounting. This is in direct contrast to the normative approach and decision-making emphasis of the conventional wisdom.

IV

Current and
Future
Developments

Agency Theory and Management Accounting

10

The purposes of this chapter are to provide an introduction to agency theory, a description of its use in management accounting research and an assessment of the contribution which researchers who are using agency theory could make to our understanding of management accounting. In view of the extent and complexity of much of the available literature only a brief description of the agency model will be provided, but this will be sufficient to establish a basis for discussing the implications of agency theory for management accounting and to indicate the explanatory nature of, at least, some current research. Although agency theory is expressed in the form of a mathematical economic model, some researchers are using it to explain observed management accounting practices.

It was pointed out in earlier chapters that during the 1970s researchers modified the economic model on which management accounting's conventional wisdom was built. These researchers introduced, first, uncertainty and, then, information costs into management accounting models. Agency theory researchers have taken this modification process a step further by adding behavioural considerations to the economic model. Although the agency model relies on marginal economic analysis, it includes explicit recognition of the behaviour of an agent (for example, a manager) whose actions the management accounting system seeks to influence or control. This modification reflects a concern for motivational issues, and brings economics-based management accounting research closer to the areas of interest of behavioural accounting researchers.

Some writers appear to believe that agency theory has the potential to provide a conceptual framework on which a comprehensive theory of management accounting could be constructed. However, it is not the contention of this chapter that agency theory offers management accounting the conceptual basis which, as argued in Chapter 2, has been lacking to date. Agency theory does not as yet (and, indeed, it is doubtful that it ever can) answer all the questions which are of interest to management accounting researchers. (Some limitations of agency models will be described later.) Nevertheless, research in this area has generated additional insights into management accounting problems and the agency theory approach appears to have replaced the 'conditional truth' approach of management accounting's conventional wisdom in much academic thinking, especially in North America.

The models used in the early information economics research in management accounting culminating in Demski and Feltham's (1976) book which was discussed in Chapter 8, were essentially concerned with single person information system choice. Although some researchers considered the problem of task specialisation, decision makers' reactions to the chosen information system were specified outside the model, rather than derived from it. In general the use of accounting information to motivate decision makers was not explored by the information economics researchers.

This limitation of the information economics approach led to some attempts at modelling information system choice using game theory. Unfortunately, game theory models can be extremely complex and there is no agreement as to the nature of the solutions in certain situations. Nevertheless, progress has been made with a particular class of these models; namely, the models set within the agency theory framework.

10.1 The Agency Theory Framework

Agency theory, as used in management accounting research, is concerned with contractual relationships between the members of a firm. The most widely used models focus on two individuals – the principal (or superior) and the agent (or subordinate). The principal delegates decision-making responsibility to the agent. Both the principal and the agent are assumed to be rational economic persons motivated solely by self-interest, but they may differ with respect to preferences, beliefs and information. The rights and responsibilities of the principal and agent are specified in a mutually agreed-upon employment contract. In management accounting research, the agency model is used to identify the combination of employment contract and information system which will maximise the utility function of the principal, subject to the behavioural constraints imposed by the self-interest of the agent.

The principal hires an agent to perform a task (which normally includes taking decisions) in an uncertain environment. The agent may be required to expend effort in the performance of this task, and the outcome will depend on both the realised state of the world and the effort expended by the agent. To maintain consistency with the symbols used to describe information economics in Chapter 8, it will be assumed that each action taken by the agent implies a different level of effort. Thus, the outcome, x, of the agent's effort (in other words, the result of selecting action, a) can be described in terms of an action/state pair, as follows:

$$x = f(s, a) \tag{10.1}$$

The agent will normally receive a reward which may be stated as a share of the outcome – the sharing rule. This sharing rule will have been agreed in drawing up the agent's employment contract. The contract will normally specify both the sharing of the outcome and the information system used to measure the outcome. Mathematically, the reward function can be expressed thus:

$$z = Z(x) \tag{10.2}$$

where z is the reward paid to the agent. The agent is assumed to derive utility from this reward, but to attach disutility to effort. Accordingly, his/her utility function can be expressed in terms of the reward received under the employment contract, less the negative effect of the effort which must be expended. This can be expressed formally in the following terms:

$$U_a(z, a) = F(z) - V(a) \tag{10.3}$$

The term, $U_a(z, a)$, represents the agent's utility function expressed in terms of reward, z, and effort, a. Remember, it is assumed that each action, a, represents a particular level of effort. Thus, the term, a, can be taken to refer either to the action or to the associated effort. It is usually assumed that the two elements of the utility function, reward and effort, are separable. As a result the positive utility for the reward can be written as $F(z)$, and the negative utility associated with effort as $V(a)$.

The principal's utility function comprises the outcome from the task, less the contracted payment to the agent. This can be expressed as follows:

$$U_p(x - z) \tag{10.4}$$

Both the principal and the agent are normally assumed to be risk-averse utility maximisers, although the principal is sometimes allowed to be risk-neutral. To simplify the exposition, it will be assumed for the present that the agent and principal share beliefs concerning the set of possible states of the world and the probabilities of each state – $s \in S$ and $\phi(s)$. Given these assumptions the principal's objective is to elicit the optimal action (or effort) from the agent, given the shared expectations concerning future states of the world. As far as the principal is concerned, the optimal action can be identified by maximising expected utility. Thus, the principal's objective function can be stated in the following terms:

$$\max_{a \in A} \sum_{s \in S} U_p(x - z)\phi(s)$$

or more fully:

$$\max_{a \in A} \sum_{s \in S} U_p(f(s,a) - Z(f(s,a)))\phi(s) \tag{10.5}$$

The principal may be able to alter the parameters of this function through the choice of (1) the information system to be used to measure the outcome, and (2) the sharing rule, both of which are embedded in the agent's employment contract. However, the principal's choice is not unrestricted. Remember the principal is attempting to influence the action that the agent is to take. It must be recognised that the agent's self-interest will also affect the action which is taken. Thus, as a first step, the principal must ensure that the utility of the reward which the agent expects to receive from the employment contract exceeds the utility that could be obtained in an alternative employment. This provides a lower limit on the expected utility for the agent. If the agent can obtain utility of $\overline{U}$ from the best alternative employment, then this constraint on the principal's actions can be written as:

$$\sum_{s \in S} F(z)\phi(s) - V(a) \geq \overline{U} \tag{10.6}$$

As the agent is assumed to be a utility maximiser, the action which he/she selects must represent an optimal action; that is, an action which maximises his/her expected utility, given the agreed employment contract. However, there will be an optimal action for the agent for each possible employment contract, i.e., for each combination of reward (sharing rule) and information system. This requirement can be expressed formally as follows:

$$a \in \text{Argmax} \sum_{s \in S} F(z)\phi(s) - V(a) \tag{10.7}$$

The expression $a \in \text{Argmax}$ indicates that the action, a, must belong to the set of optimal actions which maximise the argument which follows, namely, the agent's expected utility. Thus, the only actions which will be considered by the principal are actions which are themselves optimal as far as the agent is concerned, given the employment contract which is implied in the term $F(z)$. This condition ensures that the solution to the principal's problem is Pareto-optimal – in other words, the utility to both the agent and the principal cannot be improved without reducing the utility accruing to the other.

To summarise, the agency model set out above involves seeking an employment contract (specifying both the sharing rule and information system) which will maximise the principal's expected utility, while retaining the agent in employment and ensuring that he/she selects the optimal action, or equivalently exerts the optimal level of effort. It should be noted that although the optimal action must maximise the agent's utility function for the agreed employment contract, it need not necessarily require the maximum possible effort from the agent. An extremely high reward would probably be needed to secure the maximum effort – because of the disutility associated with effort. An employment contract with such a reward scheme may not be optimal for either the principal or the agent.

10.2 Information Asymmetry

If the principal and agent share expectations concerning the future and the principal is able to measure directly the outcome of the agent's effort then the agency model is very similar to the single person information economics model described in Chapter 8. The particular attraction of agency theory is that it is capable of exploring problems in which information is unequally distributed between the agent and the principal and/or it is impossible to directly observe the agent's effort. In the latter case, an accounting system could provide output measures from which the agent's effort may be inferred, but these measures might not accurately reflect the effort which has been expended. In other words, there may be uncertainty about the relationship between the accounting measure and the agent's effort.

If the principal cannot directly observe the agent's effort, or accurately infer it from some measure of output, then the agent may have an incentive to act in a manner which is different from what was agreed in the employment contract; for example, he may shirk. This problem is called moral hazard. Another motivational problem can arise even when the agent's effort can be directly observed. A principal who does not have access to all the information which is available to the agent at the time a decision is taken cannot know whether the effort expended has been appropriately selected on the basis of the agent's information or whether the agent has shirked. This problem is known as adverse selection.

Both moral hazard and adverse selection are the result of information asymmetries – in other words, a result of the agent and principal having different amounts of information. In management accounting research, agency theory has been used to explore the role of information (especially accounting information) in employment contracts; in particular, the role of information in improving efficiency by minimising the losses caused through problems of moral hazard and adverse selection. For this purpose, employment contracts are said to be efficient if they satisfy a Pareto-optimality criterion which states that neither party to the contract (principal nor agent) can improve his/her position at the expense of the other.

The solution technique for the agency model set out above is concerned with identifying the set of Pareto-optimal contracts. Bargaining between the principal and agent will then determine the selected contract from among this set of optimal contracts. Fortunately, however, for purposes of our discussion of the implications of agency theory for management accounting research, it is not necessary to become involved in the solution technique. The above general description of the agency model will suffice.

10.3 Limitations of the Agency Model

Before discussing the implications of agency theory, some observations are needed about the general limitations of the agency model. These limitations should be kept in mind throughout the subsequent discussion.

Tiessen and Waterhouse (1983) identified four limitations which potentially restrict the usefulness of results derived from agency models. First, the models focus on single-period behaviour. Second, the descriptive validity of a utility maximising representation of behaviour is open to question. Third, the models are generally limited to two persons. Finally, there are some writers who would argue that many business organisations are not susceptible to analysis from a formal contracting point of view. This final limitation will be discussed later when the relationship between agency theory research and 'the markets and hierarchies' literature is explored. At this point, some comments will be made about the first three limitations.

The model's single period focus allows attention to be directed towards certain issues, but suppresses many other interesting problems. Furthermore, implications derived from single-period analysis may not hold in a multi-period world. Some attempts have been made to provide solution techniques which will enable the agency model to be expressed in a multi-period form. The results of those studies which have used multi-period analysis are not quantitatively different from the results obtained using the single-period model. Thus, the single-period nature of the existing agency models may not be unduly restrictive.

The descriptive validity of the utility maximising models has been called into question by the accumulated evidence obtained from behavioural research. This evidence indicates that many individuals violate the assumptions of rational decision making in their personal behaviour. However, the importance of this evidence for decision making in an organisational context is unclear. In an organisational setting, specialisation in decision making is possible and learning through repeated exposure to similar choices may take place. Thus, rational decision making by specialist decision makers may be possible inside organisations.

While the agency problem is potentially expandable to the case of more than two people, much of the agency theory analysis of management accounting issues which will be described later has been based on two-person models. Unfortunately, the results from two-person analysis may not extend to situations where there are multiple principals and agents. The formation of coalitions and teams may require different methods of analysis and alternative solution techniques. However, there appears to be no conceptual reason why the two-person agency models used to date in management accounting research cannot be extended to include multiple agents. Some researchers have already started exploring models with two agents; for instance, in analysing problems of transfer pricing.

In general, researchers using agency theory to examine management accounting issues have tended to rely on the basic form of the agency model described above. However, recent agency theory research aimed at extending the analysis to include more complex principal–agent relationships suggests that different solutions can arise when the model is modified. According to Baiman (1990, p. 357) this research suggests that there may be implications for management accounting which have been overlooked in the literature. But as the results of agency theory research are dependent on the precise form of the agency model, it may prove very difficult to locate generalisable implications for management accounting.

A substantial part of the agency theory literature has focused on the intricacies of the mathematical analysis. Recently, however, there have been a number of empirical studies of agency models, but they have been largely concerned with financial accounting issues rather than management accounting issues. In general, these studies have been able to identify associations between management behaviour and executive compensation contracts, but they have been less successful in testing agency theory explanations of why such contracts persist. Nevertheless, some researchers have attempted to derive management accounting implications from the models which are currently available. But in view of the limitations mentioned above, care should be exercised in generalising the results beyond the simplified settings in which they were determined. Some of these implications are described below.

10.4   Some General Implications of Agency Theory

Within the agency theory framework management accounting information is used for two distinct purposes. The first use is to improve the individual's (the principal's and/or the agent's) *ex ante* assessment of the environment in which decisions have to be taken (i.e., the expected state of the world) – this is the belief revision role which was recognised in Chapter 8. The second use is to evaluate the outcomes of decisions already taken in order to facilitate the allocation of those outcomes between the principal and agent according to the terms agreed in the employment contract. This latter role, which is sometimes called the performance evaluation role, is concerned with motivating the agent to exert the optimal effort. If the agent's effort cannot be directly observed, a contract which does not link reward to performance, for example a fixed fee, will provide no incentive for effort to be exerted on the principal's behalf.

The distinction between the belief revision role and the performance evaluation role for management accounting information corresponds to a distinction between pre-decision and post-decision information. The following discussion will examine pre- and post-decision information separately. However, this should not imply that they are independent. If the ranking of information systems for pre- and post-decision purposes are not the same, then a model which examines only one of the purposes may not explain the observed use of management accounting in the more general setting where information is required for both purposes.

The role of post-decision information has received a great deal of attention in the agency theory literature. The general implications of this research will be discussed first. Subsequently, some comments will be made about the general implications of pre-decision information research, and then, particular implications for selected areas of management accounting will be mentioned.

A general issue for post-decision information research is the conditions under which one post-decision information system is strictly Pareto-superior to another. A knowledge of such conditions could help management accountants to choose between alternative accounting systems and may provide reasons to explain the observed differences in practice. Of particular interest is the question of whether a ranking of accounting systems can be achieved independently of the preferences and beliefs of the principal and agent.

It may be recalled that the information economics literature concluded that information system choice is situation specific. In the agency theory literature researchers who have examined the value (or ranking) of post-decision information systems have ignored information costs. Generally, costless information systems are considered, or at least it is assumed that there are no cost differences. It is also assumed that the information is available to both the principal and the agent.

Holmstrom (1979) demonstrated that any additional information about the agent's effort or action, however imperfect, has positive value, provided it is costlessly obtained. Furthermore, additional costless post-decision information can never give rise to a Pareto-inferior result, as the principal and agent can always agree to an employment contract which ignores that additional information. Another potentially interesting result for management accounting researchers was also found by Holmstrom (1982). An ordering of post-decision information systems, independently of the preferences and beliefs of the principal and agent involved, is possible provided the information systems concerned can be compared according to certain statistical conditions. But the question of whether or not accounting systems can be compared in this way remains problematic. Other researchers have demonstrated that an accounting performance measure, such as a profit number, may not be optimal; rather, performance evaluation should be based on separate measurements of the underlying elements (e.g., the costs and revenues) which make up the accounting profit number (Banker and Datar, 1989).

While reporting additional post-decision information can never be Pareto-inferior (i.e., it can never decrease the agent's and/or principal's utility) expanding the pre-decision information available to an agent after the contract has been agreed, but before the decision to expend effort is taken, could make the principal (and/or the agent) worse off. Such information may, on the one hand, make the agent better informed, while on the other it may relieve him/her of sufficient uncertainty concerning the outcome as to reduce his/her motivation. The net effect of these two counteracting forces will depend on the particular situation, especially the preferences and beliefs of the principal and the agent and the agent's utility function.

If the additional pre-decision information is made available to both the agent and the principal, it is possible to identify conditions for a Pareto improvement. But agency theory can offer little general guidance as to the value of pre-decision information which is available only to the agent – the most likely situation when management accounting information is involved.

The above discussion has been concerned with the general implications of agency theory and, unfortunately, offers few insights into observed management accounting practice. However, certain researchers have used the agency model to explore particular management accounting issues. Some of this work is described below.

10.5 Specific Management Accounting Implications of Agency Theory

The use of budgets, and in particular rewards based on the achievement or non-achievement of budgets, are frequently observed in practice. An interesting question for agency theory researchers is whether budget-based payments can be shown to be Pareto-optimal. Various researchers have identified conditions under which budget-based contracts are optimal, or at least Pareto-superior to other forms of contract. Unfortunately, the practical implications of these results are unclear because of the restrictive nature of the underlying assumptions used by the researchers. Holmstrom's (1979) conditions which are the most general provide some theoretical support for the observed use of budgets in practice.

Further work has demonstrated conditions for the Pareto-optimality of participation in the budgeting process. This work is generally concerned with communication between the agent and principal, rather than with participation *per se*. Nevertheless, it does provide some insights into participation. The agent can be expected to communicate with the principal, or to participate in the budgetary process, in a manner which maximises his/her expected utility. The self-interest of the agent may involve the creation of budget slack. In agency theory terms the observed phenomenon of budget slack is described as an inefficiency (or a loss) resulting from asymmetric pre-decision information.

As described in Chapter 6, the investigation of variances (from budget or standard) was studied by a number of researchers in the early 1970s. For the purpose of model development, and evaluation of those models, such as the work of Magee (1976), the researchers assumed that managers act as machines and respond impassively to signals from the investigation decision models. The agency theory framework provided researchers with an opportunity to examine managers' behavioural reactions to variance investigation models. For this purpose it is essential that information costs are not suppressed, otherwise it would be optimal to investigate either always or never.

Baiman and Demski (1980a and 1980b) demonstrated that a policy of investigating only when the observed performance is less than the budget or standard by at least a predetermined amount can be Pareto-optimal. However, much remains to be done in this area. Baiman and Demski's results are very sensitive to the particular assumptions used. Further work is needed to investigate the trigger points for investigation decisions. An evaluation of models similar to that undertaken by Magee (1976) could be usefully undertaken; but in this case, the agent (manager) could be a utility-maximising individual. Such work may provide a better explanation of the observed use of simple (for example, 1 or 2 standard deviation) decision rules.

It was suggested in Chapter 2 that responsibility accounting is central to management accounting. The conventional wisdom is that accounting reports should be prepared according to areas of responsibility and that the performance of a manager should be based on the factors which he/she can control. Agency theory confirms this interpretation of responsibility accounting only in a world of complete certainty. When uncertainty is introduced a conventional responsibility accounting system may not be Pareto-optimal.

With a risk-averse principal, the agent's performance and reward payment should not be protected from uncertainty concerning the state of the world – even if direct observation of effort is possible. An agent who is evaluated only in terms of his controllable performance – that is an agent who is isolated from the risks involved in the decisions he/she is taking – will take decisions as though he/she were risk-neutral. Such decision-taking behaviour may not maximise a (risk-averse) principal's utility function. One branch of the agency theory literature is concerned with optimal 'risk sharing'. This research suggests that, unless the principal is risk-neutral, Pareto-optimality requires the agent to absorb at least some of the risk associated with the possible outcomes. Risk sharing can be achieved by relating part or all of the agent's reward to the actual outcome, without any adjustment for changes in the state of the world. This will mean that the agent's expected utility will depend on his/her assessment of the state possibilities. Accordingly, the agent will consider the risks involved in the decisions being taken.

If only imperfect post-decision information can be obtained (i.e., information which does not accurately reflect the agent's effort or the desired outcome) all available information should be used to learn as much as possible about the agent's action/effort.

This may involve assessing the agent's performance on the basis of information concerning outcomes over which he/she cannot exercise complete control. Such evaluations are frequently observed in practice; for instance, allocations of joint and common costs can introduce non-controllable elements into performance reports. Zimmerman's explanation for the widespread use of cost allocations in practice were mentioned in Chapter 9. However, Zimmerman did not show that cost allocations can be Pareto-optimal. As we will discuss later, he demonstrated only that a change in the fixed component of an agent's reward payment can affect his/her motivation. He did not rigorously analyse the link between the sharing rule and cost allocations. In a more comprehensive analysis, Demski (1981) found that any information value which arises from cost allocations derives from the measurement of the activity variables on which the allocation is based. No value arises from the cost allocation itself.

Baiman (1982) conjectured that a multi-period, multi-person agency framework is likely to be needed to explain cost allocations. Within the two-person, single-period agency model cost allocation appears just as irrational as within management accounting's conventional wisdom. However, using a two-agent (one principal) model, Suh (1987 and 1988) has demonstrated that allocations of non-controllable costs may be necessary where there is collusion between the agents, where one of the agents has private information which is costly to communicate to the principal, or where there is correlation between the non-controllable costs and the performance of the individual agents. Furthermore, Baiman and Noel (1985) demonstrated that in a multi-period agency model it could be optimal to allocate capacity costs (such as depreciation) to an agent, even when such costs are completely uncontrollable by the agent. Thus, agency models may offer some explanations for cost allocations.

The purpose of this discussion of agency theory is not to provide a complete rationalisation of management accounting practice. Rather, it is intended to demonstrate that agency theory has the potential to explain some observed practices, and more particularly, that management accounting researchers recognise this explanatory role. The above brief review of the implications of agency theory research provides some examples of how the change of emphasis in management accounting research identified in

Chapter 9 has influenced researchers' attitudes towards the relationship between normative models and observed practice. The explanation of existing practice is now an important test of normative theory.

10.6 The Contribution of Agency Theory

The earlier sections of this chapter have attempted to show that agency theory is a potentially useful tool for management accounting research. In particular, it yields practical implications, especially in the areas of budgeting (including participation) and variance investigations. But the limitations of the highly simplified settings of agency models should be recognised in any attempts to generalise these implications. However, researchers are now beginning to make progress beyond the simple two-person, single-period models.

Much of the analysis to date has been at the theoretical level. Mathematical conditions for the optimality of certain observed practices have been stated, but without empirical support. These mathematical conditions imply a set of circumstances in which observed practices could be optimal. Empirical research is needed to test whether the occurrence of observed practice corresponds to these prescribed circumstances. Walker (1989) has argued that such tests will not be easy to design because of the difficulties of stating the mathematical conditions in the form of testable hypotheses. Such tests are essential, however, if agency theory is to provide implications beyond the present superficial statements that particular observed practices could be optimal.

Some researchers are now beginning to conduct behavioural experiments to explore particular aspects of the agency model. However, these experiments are generally based on highly simplified decision settings and use students as experimental subjects. Such studies have found some support for agency theory analyses. But it is far from clear whether similar results will be found in studies of much more complex organisational decision processes. Nevertheless, the agency framework does offer some new insights into the nature of management accounting. In particular, it has emphasised management accounting's role as a control system, as well as a decision facilitating system which was the primary concern of earlier research. This new emphasis has led to a recognition of the importance of accounting information in the motivation of organisational participants and of the need to consider the behavioural responses of such participants in designing and choosing accounting systems. Managers can no longer be considered passive reactors to signals from information systems. They can be expected to modify their behaviour in response to information according to their personal beliefs, needs and desires. Thus, behavioural issues are beginning to influence the quantitative, economic-based research in management accounting.

Agency theory has also emphasised the importance of 'risk sharing' in the design of accounting systems. This runs contrary to the conventional wisdom of management accounting which sought to isolate managers from the effects of uncertainty. An important distinction is made in the agency theory literature between *ex ante* and *ex post* uncertainty. *Ex post* uncertainty arises because of imperfections in information systems. Such uncertainty may be inevitable because of the high costs of obtaining accurate measures of relevant factors. An optimal sharing of this uncertainty is essential for the motivation of agents (managers).

Some writers have argued that agency theory could provide the basis for a comprehensive theory of management accounting, for example, Baiman (1982) and Sundem (1981). However, others believe that the complexities of modern organisations will defy modelling in such a structured way, for example, Spicer and Ballew (1983). Only the future will tell which view is correct. However, agency theory research has provided an additional dimension to our understanding of management accounting issues. But other approaches may add further dimensions and should not be ignored. Agency theory cannot be viewed as the only possible way of approaching management accounting problems, although it is an approach which has currently found favour in certain academic journals.

It is only by undertaking research on a broad front that progress will be made towards a better understanding of management accounting. An alternative, or possibly a complement, to agency theory is provided by the economics of internal organisation literature and, in particular, the markets and hierarchies approach of Oliver Williamson. Although the work of Williamson is sometimes regarded as an antecedent to agency theory, Spicer and Ballew (1983) argued that agency theory is a special case of

Williamson's organisation failures framework (see Williamson, 1975, Chapter 2).

An organisation failure is said to occur when the costs associated with one mode of organising transactions (for example, a market) would be reduced by shifting those transactions to an alternative organisational arrangement (for example, the internal hierarchy of a firm). From a management accounting perspective attention can be focused on the transaction costs involved in allocating resources within the firm. It can be argued that the high costs of market-related transactions can be avoided by developing an internal constitution, either explicitly or implicitly, which specifies the general rules of co-operative behaviour within a firm. A study of the nature of such internal constitutions may give insights into the issues of resource allocation in a multi-period, multi-person organisational setting.

Many of the issues addressed by agency theory researchers, such as uncertainty, information asymmetry, adverse selection and moral hazard, can be examined within the organisation failures framework. However, the economics of internal organisation literature generally adopts the bounded rationality concept of economic behaviour (rather than utility maximisation) and the analysis is far less structured than agency theory. It has been claimed that the organisation failures framework provides an explanatory theory of economic organisation (Spicer and Ballew, 1983). Historical studies have shown that hierarchical business organisations developed as a substitute for the more costly market-based mechanisms of resource allocation (Chandler, 1977; Chandler and Daems, 1980; and Johnson, 1980 and 1983).

Tiessen and Waterhouse (1983) attempted to reconcile agency theory and the organisation failures framework within the context of a contingency model of organisations. In a highly structured and predictable environment with routine technologies it may be possible to write highly specific contracts of the form analysed by agency theory researchers. But when the environment or technology is non-routine or very uncertain such contracts will be infeasible and the organisation failures framework may provide a more appropriate mode of analysis.

Some insights provided by agency theory were described above. The economics of internal organisation may offer further insights, but as yet few specific implications for management accounting have been generated, although writers such as Spicer and Ballew (1983) and Tiessen and Waterhouse (1983) have made some general observations. The economics of internal organisation literature is clearly concerned with explanatory theories, whilst the agency theory literature is primarily normative. Nevertheless, both attach importance to explaining observed management accounting practice. To finish this chapter we will look at some explanations which have been given for cost allocations.

10.7 Possible Reasons for Cost Allocations

As mentioned in Chapter 9, Zimmerman (1979) argued that as overheads are frequently allocated in practice, it is likely that the technique yields benefits which exceed the costs involved. Rather than criticising practitioners for not adopting the cost allocation techniques developed in the research literature, Zimmerman elected to explore possible explanations for the observed widespread occurrence of particular practices. However, his paper provides only suggestions or possible reasons for allocations rather than a rigorous theoretical explanation of them. Zimmerman's suggestions proceeded along two quite distinct lines.

The first suggestion is that allocations are used to provide approximations for opportunity costs. As an illustration, consider pricing decisions. Economic theory indicates that in setting prices decision makers should ensure that sales revenues are sufficient to cover long run marginal costs. But in the long run all costs are marginal costs, including costs which, in the short run, can be regarded as fixed costs. Therefore, such 'fixed costs' have to be recognised in any attempt to measure long run marginal cost. Although the allocations used in practice do not necessarily lead to accurate measures of long run marginal cost, they may provide reasonable approximations. Furthermore, the information costs which would be incurred in obtaining more accurate measures of the appropriate long run marginal costs may considerably outweigh the gains which would be obtained from having such information.

Allocations may also be used to provide an approximate measure of the opportunity costs needed for short run decisions concerning the use of existing productive capacity. It could be very expensive or quite impracticable to measure accurately the opportunity costs of using available machines at various levels of activity. Accordingly, allocations of depreciation charges may provide reasonable approximations, i.e., approximations which are cost efficient in terms of the costs and benefits of the information. More accurate measures of opportunity costs may be possible theoretically, for instance by using techniques such as linear programming, but the cost of such information may exceed its benefits. However, as information costs are situation specific (see Chapter 8), no general conclusions can be drawn. Each situation must be considered separately. Nevertheless, this suggestion could explain the widespread use of cost allocations in practice. But empirical research is needed to assess the costs and benefits of such uses of cost allocations.

The second suggestion offered by Zimmerman involves considering a manager in the role of an agent. The owner of the business or a senior manager (the principal) often delegates decision-making responsibility to a subordinate manager (the agent). In a business setting such delegated decisions involve choices about the activities which are undertaken with a view to earning profits and, within limits, choices about how those profits will be distributed. It is argued in the agency theory literature that if surplus profits are available, a manager (the agent) may divert them into perks for himself/herself, rather than reporting them as profits for his/her department. A manager may obtain greater satisfaction from such perks as luxurious offices, well-qualified assistants, company cars, etc., than he/she would get from the rewards associated with reporting higher profits.

Zimmerman argued that an allocation of central management overhead could reduce the surplus profits which might be available to a manager and, thus, such allocations would limit the manager's ability to divert resources into perks for himself/herself. Although this explanation was not rigorously developed, it represented a first attempt at using the agency theory framework to study cost allocations. As we discussed above, other researchers have refined the use of the agency theory framework. The important point to highlight is that these researchers do not dismiss existing practices in constructing their theory. This contrasts markedly with recent developments in the cost allocation literature, which we will discuss in the next two chapters.

Cost Allocation Models 11

In the past there have been many criticisms of the use of allocations in the practice of management accounting. As discussed in Chapter 2, the conventional wisdom of management accounting is that all allocations are arbitrary. But, as was pointed out in Chapter 3, allocations are widespread in practice. To use the words of Dopuch (1981, p. 6) 'too much cost allocation has been carried out in practice to lead us to believe it is all bad'. Consequently, cost allocations have become a focal point for discussions of the gap between theory and practice.

Over the years researchers interested in cost allocations have concentrated on prescriptive models, i.e., models which indicate how allocations ought to be made. Some researchers have accepted the arguments that allocations are necessary (even arbitrary), but argue that if practitioners want to use them, researchers should attempt to identify the best methods to use in particular circumstances.

Recently, both researchers and practitioners have expressed concern over the methods of cost allocation which are used in practice. This concern has led to questions about the usefulness of product cost information and, in particular, whether inaccurate product costs due to inappropriate allocation methods are undermining the competitiveness of Western businesses *vis-à-vis* their Japanese competitors. Here it is not the use of allocations *per se* which is being questioned, but the methods of allocation actually used. New cost allocation methods have been developed, and it is claimed that they will improve product cost information.

In this chapter we will examine briefly conventional textbook methods of cost allocation and then review some of the models which have been proposed by researchers over the years. This will provide relevant background for a discussion in the next chapter of new methods of cost allocation; in particular, activity-based costing which is currently attracting the interest of both researchers and practitioners of management accounting.

11.1 The Textbook Approach

Cost allocations are concerned with the partitioning of costs among a number of cost objects. Traditionally, cost objects have included departments, cost centres (such as individual machines or productive processes), particular products and groups of products. In essence, cost allocations are concerned with situations in which a particular cost is allocated to two or more cost objects. In describing such allocations most textbooks distinguish joint costs and common costs. Although both types of cost involve allocations, they give rise to different problems.

Joint products arise whenever a single resource or production process is used to produce two or more outputs. In such a situation, the input costs are incurred in the joint production of the several products. The classic example is the meat packer who, from a single resource (such as a cow), produces various grades and types of meat in addition to the hide which can be used for leather, various by-products such as bones and fat which can be used in certain productive processes, such as the production of glue, and a whole variety of other items. Joint cost allocation is concerned with partitioning the cost of the cow among the individual cost objects, i.e., the various products which are produced. It is relatively easy to think of many similar joint product situations, e.g., dairy products, oil refining, other refining and chemical processes, telephone companies and even universities which provide both teaching and research.

Common costs arise when a particular intermediate product or service is used by two or more users within the firm. A good example of common costs is the provision of centralised computer services. These services will be provided to a variety of departments and/or divisions. Other illustrations include the costs of centrally produced power and electricity, research and development, accounting services and general administration. Common costs are frequently allocated to the user departments and in some instances the users have the option of either using these centrally provided services or going outside the organisation to obtain similar services. Thus, the allocations of these common costs may be regarded as the prices for the internally produced service, and in this sense they are very similar to the transfer prices which are used for intermediate products in multi-divisional organisations. In fact, many of the principles which are associated with the allocation of common costs also apply to transfer prices.

As described in Chapter 2 the economic approach to decision making which forms the basis of management accounting's conventional wisdom relies on the concept of marginal cost. According to this approach, decisions should be based on comparisons of marginal costs and marginal revenues. It is argued that allocations can distort the decision-making process if they generate cost information which does not reflect marginal costs. Cost allocations involve the partitioning of total costs and normally lead to average rather than marginal cost. As a result, it is difficult to justify allocations of total costs in terms of information for decision making, at least in the context of management accounting's conventional wisdom. But as we will discuss in Chapter 12 this view is coming under increasing criticism.

Most textbooks argue that allocations are needed for a variety of purposes, such as inventory valuations for financial reporting, product costings especially for 'full price' contracts (required by a variety of bodies including many government agencies) and also for decision making concerning the provision or use of the service, resource, etc. which gives rise to the cost. It was this last need for allocations which attracted the attention of researchers in the 1970s and early 1980s. However, recently the need for product cost information has become the focus of attention of cost allocation researchers. The objective of this current research is to identify as accurately as possible the *total* cost of producing individual products. Previously, however, the general approach to cost allocations in the research literature was first to identify marginal costs associated with particular cost objects and then to allocate the fixed costs in a manner which as far as possible would not distort the decision making process. In the following sections of this chapter we will look first at the prescriptions that this previous research contained for the allocation of joint costs and then at the prescriptions for the allocation of common costs.

11.2 Allocations of Joint Costs

As mentioned above, joint costs arise when a single resource or productive process is used to produce two or more outputs. The cost allocation problem is concerned with allocating the resource and/or production costs to the individual products. The essence of a joint cost problem, however, is that the products are inextricably linked – one product cannot be produced without the other product(s). In practice, the individual products may be further processed individually. The point at which the joint products become separately identifiable is known as the 'split-off point'. It is the costs incurred up to this point which are known as joint costs. The subsequent costs can be identified and charged directly to the individual products.

The joint cost allocation method most commonly advocated in textbooks is the net realisable value method. Under this method the joint costs are allocated to individual products in proportion to their net realisable value. If a product can be sold at the split-off point (whether or not it is sold does not matter) its net realisable value is the selling price less any selling costs at that point. The net realisable value of a product which has no market value at the split-off point is the selling price after further processing, less the further processing costs and any subsequent selling costs.

The principal attraction of the net realisable value method is that it ensures that all the joint products are profitable when the joint production process as a whole is profitable. It avoids situations in which there might be a temptation to terminate production of individual products when their joint production is still worthwhile. However, the allocations do not in general provide information which will lead to optimal product mix or output decisions.

Furthermore, since the net realisable value method requires information concerning selling prices, these allocations cannot be used for subsequent price setting.

Some researchers have proposed avoiding joint cost allocations altogether for purposes of decision making. Because the products are inextricably linked in the production process, such researchers argue that it is necessary to consider the process as a whole in order to reach product mix and output decisions. For example, Hartley (1971) used the following information to illustrate decision making when joint products are involved.

Products A and B are produced jointly from the same raw material. Each unit of the raw material will yield three units of product A and two units of product B. The costs of the raw material and the joint processing of the two products amounts to £2 per unit of raw material. Both products can either be sold at the split-off point or further processed. In the case of product A, it can be sold at split-off for £8, or further processed at a cost of £6 and then sold at £15. Product B, however, can be sold at split-off for £7, or further processed at a cost of £4 and then sold for £10. This information is summarised in Table 11.1. As can be seen, product A has a positive contribution of £1 from further processing, whereas product B has a loss of £1 from such processing. As might be expected, the analysis described below suggests that product B should be sold entirely at the split-off point and not further processed. The problem for the decision maker is to decide how much raw material to process, and how much of each product to sell at the split-off point and how much to process further.

Hartley (1971) described the solution to this decision problem using a linear programming approach. The linear programme is set out in Table 11.2, where the relevant variables are defined. The objective function is expressed in terms of maximising total contribution from the production and sale of the two products. However, there are five variables in the objective function. Because each product can be sold either at split-off or after further processing, two variables are required for each product. In addition, there is a variable representing the raw material input. In the case of product A, sale at the split-off point will generate a contribution of £8, whereas sale after further processing will generate a contribution of £9. In the case of product B, the respective contributions are £7 and £6. However, the cost of the

TABLE 11.1
Information for Illustration of Joint Product Decision Making

	Products	
	A	B
Market value after additional processing	£ 15	£ 10
Cost of additional processing	6	4
Contribution of additional processing	9	6
Market value at split-off	8	7
Advantage (disadvantage) of additional processing	£ 1	£ (1)

SOURCE   Hartley (1971) p. 747.

TABLE 11.2
Linear Programme for Joint Product Decision Making

Maximise: $\quad 8x_1 + 9x_2 + 7x_3 + 6x_4 - 2x_5$

Subject to:

$$
\begin{aligned}
x_5 &\leqslant 40\,000 \\
3x_2 + x_4 + 1.5x_5 &\leqslant 80\,000 \\
x_1 + x_2 - 3x_5 &\leqslant 0 \\
x_3 + x_4 - 2x_5 &\leqslant 0 \\
x_1, \quad x_2, \quad x_3, \quad x_4, \quad x_5 &\geqslant 0
\end{aligned}
$$

where x_1 = quantity of product A sold at the split-off point,
$\quad\ \ x_2$ = quantity of product A sold after additional processing,
$\quad\ \ x_3$ = quantity of product B sold at the split-off point,
$\quad\ \ x_4$ = quantity of product B sold after additional processing,
$\quad\ \ x_5$ = quantity of raw material used in production.

raw material must be deducted from these contributions earned.
Each unit of the raw material costs £2. Using the definitions given
in Table 11.2, the objective function can be written as follows:

$$\text{Maximise: } 8x_1 + 9x_2 + 7x_3 + 6x_4 - 2x_5 \qquad (11.1)$$

The objective function is constrained, however, by the availability of raw materials, the available machine time, and the relationship between the joint products and the raw material input. The first constraint expresses the availability of the raw material:

$$x_5 \leqslant 40\,000 \tag{11.2}$$

The raw material used should not exceed the available quantity of $40\,000$ units. The next constraint relates to the machine time available for production. $80\,000$ machine hours are available and can be used either in the joint production process or in the further processing of products A and B. One and a half hours is required for each unit of the raw material used in the joint production process, whereas three hours and one hour are required for the further processing of products A and B. This constraint is written as:

$$3x_2 + x_4 + 1.5x_5 \leqslant 80\,000 \tag{11.3}$$

The next two constraints in Table 11.2 specify the required relationship between the raw material input and the outputs of the joint production process. Each unit of raw material produces three units of product A. Thus, the quantity of product A sold at split-off and after further processing cannot exceed three times the raw material used in production.
Mathematically:

$$x_1 + x_2 \leqslant 3x_5 \tag{11.4}$$

This equation is rearranged for Table 11.2. Likewise, the relationship between the raw material and product B can be written as follows:

$$x_3 + x_4 \leqslant 2x_5 \tag{11.5}$$

and rearranged for the purposes of Table 11.2. Finally the non-negativity constraints are specified to complete the formulation of the linear programme.
This linear programme can be solved manually, but most likely a computer package will be used. The solution is set out in Table

11.3. As expected, product B is not subjected to further processing. 40 000 units of the raw material are used to produce 80 000 units of product B and 120 000 units of product A. Whereas all the units of B are sold at the split-off point, $6\,666\,\frac{2}{3}$ units of product A are subjected to further processing.

TABLE 11.3
Solution to Joint Product Decision Problem

Total contribution earned	£ 1 446 667
Product A sold at split-off	$113\,333\frac{1}{3}$
Product A sold after further processing	$6\,666\frac{2}{3}$
Product B sold at split-off	80 000
Product B sold after further processing	0
Raw material used in production	40 000

Hartley added a number of extensions to his illustration to cope with such things as market constraints and variable proportions (i.e., the possibility of varying the ratio of products A and B). While these extensions add to the complexity of the mathematical model, they do not involve any change in basic principles. In addition, Jensen (1973) introduced the notion of demand curves into the analysis. This extension allows prices to vary with output, but requires a non-linear programming technique to arrive at a solution. However, once again there are no fundamentally new principles involved, but there is a spin-off. In certain cases, the dual prices which are obtained in the solution of such a problem can be used to allocate the joint costs.

Kaplan (1982) provided an illustration of such a situation. Consider a joint production problem in which two units of product 1 and one unit of product 2 can be obtained for each unit of a particular raw material. The selling prices of the two products, denoted p_1 and p_2, are influenced by the quantity of each which is sold. If we let these quantities be x_1 and x_2, the demand curve for the two products can be written as follows:

$$x_1 = \frac{49 - p_1}{2} \tag{11.6}$$

$$x_2 = 15 - p_2 \tag{11.7}$$

Unlimited quantities of the raw material can be obtained at a price of £3 per unit and the variable processing costs are £2 per unit produced. Kaplan (1982) demonstrated a solution to the problem of determining the amount of raw material to process and the output and price of the two products.

If we assume that neither product can be further processed, the gross revenue from sales of the two products can be written as follows:

$$\text{Gross revenue} = x_1 p_1 + x_2 p_2 \tag{11.8}$$

If the demand functions in equations (11.6) and (11.7) are rearranged and introduced into equation (11.8), the gross revenue can be rewritten as follows:

$$\begin{aligned}
\text{Gross revenue} &= x_1(49 - 2x_1) + x_2(15 - x_2) \\
&= 49x_1 - 2x_1^2 + 15x_2 - x_2^2
\end{aligned} \tag{11.9}$$

Finally, if we let z represent the amount of raw material used in production, the production costs amount to $5z$. Thus, the objective function for this decision problem can be expressed as follows:

$$\text{Maximise: } 49x_1 - 2x_1^2 + 15x_2 - x_2^2 - 5z \tag{11.10}$$

This objective function is subject to the constraints imposed by the relationship between the two products and the input of raw material. These constraints can be written as $x_1 = 2z$ and $x_2 = z$. Kaplan expresses these constraints as inequalities rather than as equalities. However, his solution technique involves converting the inequalities into equalities. The formulation of the problem is set out in Table 11.4. Kaplan demonstrated that the solution to this problem is to produce 12 units of product 1 (which can be sold at £25 each) and 6 units of product 2 (which can be sold at £9 each). In arriving at this solution, he deduced the following allocation of the £5 joint costs:

£2 to the two units of product 1, and
£3 to the one unit of product 2.

TABLE 11.4
A Non-Linear Joint Product Decision Problem

$$\text{Maximise:} \quad 49x_1 \ - \ 2x_1^2 \ + \ 15x_2 \ - \ x_2^2 \ - \ 5z$$
$$\text{Subject to:} \qquad\qquad x_1 \ \leqslant \ 2z$$
$$x_2 \ \leqslant \ z$$
$$x_1, x_2, z \ \geqslant \ 0$$

SOURCE   Kaplan (1982).

This allocation, he argued, can be used to decentralise the decision-making process. If decisions concerning products 1 and 2 are taken separately, by different decision makers, then optimal decisions will result, provided the joint costs are allocated in the manner described.

Thus, it is possible to determine simultaneously the optimum output and price decisions and the joint cost allocation. However, it is reasonable to ask whether such allocations are really very useful, as the optimal decisions have already been determined. These allocated costs may be useful for assessing small variations from the optimal plan; for instance, the purchase of additional amounts of the raw material or the productive services. But it must be emphasised that, as with all dual prices, the cost information is valid only for small changes around the optimal plan. Finally, it should be pointed out that these joint cost allocations apply only to the variable joint costs. Fixed costs would normally not be included in the mathematical formulation. Allocations of joint fixed costs (overheads) can be treated in the same way as allocations of common costs.

An early paper, by Kaplan and Thompson (1971), demonstrated that mathematical programming can be used to allocate overheads in such a way that identical decisions will be made before and after the allocation. The first step in their approach is to formulate and solve a linear programming problem as described above. The associated dual prices can then be used to determine the opportunity costs of the scarce resources used in the production process. The overheads will then be allocated in proportion to these opportunity costs. This has the effect of preserving the relative profitability of individual products and ensuring that a linear programming formulation which included such allocated costs will lead to the same solution as was obtained from the original formulation. This approach provides an important principle which has been followed by many researchers interested in allocations of common costs, namely the allocation of common costs should be neutral with respect to decision making. In other words, although allocations may be unnecessary, if they are used they should not distort the decision-making process.

11.3 Allocations of Common Costs

Whereas joint cost allocations are concerned with allocating costs across products, common costs are usually allocated across the departments, divisions, etc., which are the ultimate users of the product or service concerned. As indicated in Chapter 3, such allocations are frequently observed in practice. The conventional wisdom of management accounting is that such allocations are unnecessary if they relate to fixed costs, but variable costs should be allocated on some appropriate basis. When actual firms are asked why they allocate common costs, responses such as 'to remind profit centre managers that (common) costs exist and that profit centre earnings must be adequate to cover those costs' and 'to fairly reflect each profit centre's usage of essential common services' are frequently obtained (Fremgen and Liao, 1981). However, few firms appear to allocate fixed and variable costs separately.

Many textbooks distinguish fixed costs and variable costs for purposes of allocation. It is usually argued that the allocation of variable costs should be based on the amount of the service actually used, whereas the fixed costs can (should) be allocated on the basis of the capacity provided to render those services. Nevertheless, it is usually admitted that even if such principles are applied, the choice of allocation base is quite arbitrary. A number of common allocation bases are illustrated in Table 11.5.

Despite the arbitrariness of these allocations, much of the early research on the topic (as reflected in current textbooks) concentrated on achieving mathematical accuracy, especially in the allocation of service department costs. The particular problem

TABLE 11.5
Some Common Allocation Bases

Cost	Base for variable cost	Base for fixed costs
Central power plant	Actual consumption	Budget cost at budgeted capacity
Personnel department	Average number of employees Labour hours worked	Labour hours at budgeted capacity
Computer services	Computer time used	Budgeted/expected usage
Central buying	Cost of material purchased Number of orders issued	Budgeted material cost
Canteen	Average number of employees	Budgeted employees
Maintenance department	Machine hours worked	Machine hours at budgeted capacity

frequently considered arises in situations where service departments provide services to each other as well as to the production departments.

The simplest way of dealing with this problem is to ignore it. The costs of the service departments can be allocated directly to the production departments – the *direct method*. The provision of services by one service department to another is ignored under this method. The *step-down method*, however, allows for a partial recognition of these services. The first step under this method is to identify the costs associated with the service department which provides the highest proportion of its services to other service departments. The cost of this department is then allocated to other service departments and to the production departments. The next and subsequent steps involve selecting the service department with the next highest proportion and allocating its costs (including costs allocated at previous steps) to the remaining service departments and the production departments. Service departments whose costs have already been allocated are ignored, and the process continues until the costs of all service departments have been allocated.

Unfortunately, both these methods ignore the essential problem of the simultaneity of the service provision. Most textbooks demonstrate that it is possible to make simultaneous allocations using a method known as the *reciprocal method*. This involves constructing a set of mathematical equations to model the relationships between the costs of the various service and production departments – one equation for each service department. Solving these equations simultaneously yields the figures needed to allocate the service department costs to the production departments.

The use of the reciprocal method yields allocations which appear to be very logical and precise. However, the actual allocations depend entirely on the choice of the allocation bases and these choices can be quite arbitrary. The arbitrariness of the allocations may be masked by the apparent mathematical precision of the reciprocal method. The differences in the allocations resulting from using an *ad hoc* mathematical method, such as the step-down method, rather than the more accurate reciprocal method, may be quite trivial when compared to the differences which could be caused by using alternative allocation bases. Accordingly, attempts to achieve mathematical accuracy may be quite futile exercises.

There is no guarantee that any particular allocation base will result in allocations which reflect the opportunity cost of the service. But as service department costs are allocated to the users of the service, they may influence decisions concerning those services, e.g., the quantity of service used and whether the service should be obtained from an alternative source (where the decision maker has authority to do so). This has encouraged researchers to consider the effect of common cost allocations on decisions to use the services concerned.

Moriarty (1975) argued that services are provided centrally when it is more efficient, or cheaper, to provide them in that way, rather than for each department to provide the services independently. Thus he argues: 'rather than allocate costs directly to a cost object, it should be possible to allocate the cost savings as an offset to the cost of obtaining services independently' (1975, p. 792).

The basic equation of Moriarity's allocation method is set out in Table 11.6. The method involves determining the minimum alternative cost which a department would incur if the services were not provided centrally. Assume that, at present, there is a common cost of CC incurred centrally and that each department has to incur a further incremental cost of I. The minimum alternative cost to any department would be the lower of: (1) the cost which the department would incur if it obtained the services independently from an outside source, Y, and (2) the cost which would be incurred if it took over the common costs itself and continued to incur its incremental cost, $CC + I$. In Table 11.6 this minimum alternative cost is represented by W. The total cost savings to the organisation can be determined by summing these alternative costs for all the departments and subtracting the costs which are currently incurred, i.e., the common cost and the sum of the incremental costs incurred by the departments. Moriarity proposes allocating this cost saving to the various departments in proportion to their minimum alternative costs. The allocated cost saving for department i is the term in the square bracket in Table 11.6.

TABLE 11.6
Moriarity Allocation

$$M_i = W_i - \left[\frac{W_i}{\sum_j W_j} \left(\sum_j W_j - \left(CC + \sum_j I_j \right) \right) \right] - I_i$$

where

M_i = common cost allocated to department i,

W_i = minimum cost alternative available to department i for the common good or service
= min $(Y_i, CC + I_i)$,

Y_i = cost at which department i could have obtained the common good or service independently,

CC = common cost,

I_i = incremental cost incurred by department i when there is a common provision of the good or service.

Moriarity's allocation is then computed by subtracting the cost saving attributable to a department and the incremental cost which the department must incur from the minimum alternative cost for that department. Thus, the allocation comprises the alternative cost which a department would incur less a share of the cost saving from having the services provided centrally (and, of course, less its incremental costs).

TABLE 11.7
Moriarity Allocation of £400 Common Costs

Department i	Independent costs Y_i	Incremental costs I_i	Minimum alternative costs W_i	Allocated cost saving *	Moriarity allocation M_i	Total costs incurred $M_i + I_i$
Production	£1 000	£490	£890	£8.17	£391.83	£881.83
Offices	200	190	200	1.83	8.17	198.17
	£1 200	* £680	£1 090	£10.00	£400.00	£1 080.00

$$* \quad \frac{W_i}{\sum\limits_{j} W_j} \left(\sum_{j} W_j - \left(CC + \sum_{j} I_j \right) \right).$$

Table 11.7 provides a numerical illustration of Moriarity's allocation. In this case, £400 of common costs are to be allocated to the production department and the offices. These costs are incurred in providing cleaning services for the two departments. However, the total costs of cleaning the two departments amount to £1 080. This amount comprises the £400 common costs and identifiable incremental costs of £490 for production and £190 for the offices. If the common services were not provided, the production department estimates that it could obtain the services independently at a cost of £1 000, whereas the estimate for the offices is only £200.

Using these figures the minimum alternative cost for the production department is £890. It would be worthwhile for that department to bear the whole of the £400 common cost and pay its existing incremental costs of £490; the total of £890 is less than the independent cost of £1 000. However, in the case of the offices, the minimum cost would be incurred by acquiring the independent services at £200. Thus, the two departments together have minimum alternative costs of £1 090. As the total costs are currently £1 080, there is a cost saving of £10 to be allocated. This is allocated on the basis of 890/1090 to the production department, and 200/1090 to the offices. The cost allocation can now be completed by subtracting these cost savings and the incremental costs for each department from the minimum alternative costs. The allocations to the production department and the offices are shown in Table 11.7.

This approach provides the decision maker with a means of comparing the cost of the common service with the cost of the next best alternative. Assuming that the provision of a common service is efficient, then each department should not bear more than the cost of the next best alternative. Accordingly, all the departments should be encouraged to continue using the common services. However, a considerable amount of information is needed centrally to compute these allocations. Much of this information (e.g., the independent costs and the incremental costs) must be provided by the departments concerned. As a result, departments might have incentives to inflate such cost information in order to reduce their allocation.

Furthermore, in certain circumstances Moriarity's allocation procedure can result in negative amounts being allocated to particular departments. For example, the illustration in Table 11.8, which is adapted from Biddle and Steinberg (1984), has a negative allocation for department 3. This could result in departments 1 and 2 attempting to exclude department 3 from the common service. Although solutions have been suggested to overcome this problem, it raises a fundamental issue. These allocation procedures focus on the individual decision maker, whereas common costs arise in situations where there are groups of decision makers co-operating in the provision and use of a common service. The recognition of this issue has caused some

TABLE 11.8
Moriarity Allocation Applied to a Three-Department Firm with £500 Common Costs

Department i	Independent costs Y_i	Incremental costs I_i	Minimum alternative costs W_i	Allocated cost saving *	Moriarity allocation M_i	Total costs incurred M_i+I_i
1	£400	£50	£400	£120	£230	£280
2	700	100	600	180	320	420
3	1 000	750	1 000	300	−50	700
	£2 100	£900	£2 000	£600	£500	£1400

$$* \quad \frac{W_i}{\sum_j W_j} \left(\sum_j W_j - \left(CC + \sum_j I_j \right) \right).$$

researchers to look to game theory to provide a mathematical basis for cost allocations, as will be discussed below.

11.4   Other Approaches

Cost allocations were quite popular in the research literature in the late 1970s. Many of the papers used a game theory approach, which had been proposed somewhat earlier – Shubik (1962). This approach treats the departments using a central service as the participants in a 'game'. As the actions of individual players (departments), such as using more or less of the service, or obtaining the service from outside the firm, could affect other players in the game, the procedures for allocating the common costs and revenues (and thus profit) are designed to provide incentives for joint actions which maximise firm-wide profits. However, in order to develop such allocation procedures, the game theory models begin with a set of axioms which the allocation is expected to achieve.

Without going into the mathematical detail of these axioms, they have been characterised as requiring fair, equitable and neutral allocations – fair and equitable to all participants in the game and neutral as far as decision-making processes are concerned. However, the notions of fairness and equity which are embodied in game theory approaches to cost allocation have been imposed by the researchers. Individual managers and even other researchers may disagree with them. In practice, it may prove difficult to establish universally acceptable notions of fairness and equity. Thus, the use of game theory based on a set of allocation axioms may not solve the arbitrariness issue in as much as the axioms themselves may be arbitrary. Banker (1981) proposed a revised set of axioms which lead to alternative allocation procedures. He claims that his axioms are superior to those conventionally used in the cost allocation literature. But there is no logical basis for selecting a particular set of axioms.

The game theory approach adds a substantial element of complexity to the cost allocation issue, but takes us no closer to an understanding of cost allocations in practice. The approach takes the need for allocations as given and attempts to develop procedures which ensure co-operative behaviour leading to firm-wide profit maximisation. Each decision maker is assumed to be concerned to advance the interests of his/her department, and the allocations are used to ensure that such interests will be served only through the required co-operative behaviour.

A similar, but far less rigorous, approach has been proposed by Bodnar and Lusk (1977). They argue that allocations can be used to encourage particular behaviours, including behaviours which may not be easily measured in financial terms. For instance, they use the illustration of a university which wants to encourage its academic departments to pursue research and to generate publications. They suggest that costs and/or revenues could be allocated in such a way as to favour departments with the greater numbers of publications. Thus, a department with a good publications record would receive more funds or a smaller allocation of costs than a department with a poor publications record. Such financial incentives are intended to encourage departments to undertake the necessary research in order to obtain the required publications record.

Such procedures could be applied to any type of desired behaviour in any organisation. However, it must be recognised that these allocations do not indicate the opportunity cost of the behaviour concerned. They simply draw attention to certain objectives and give encouragement to particular behaviours.

Most of the approaches discussed in this chapter have taken the need for allocations as given. In many instances, allocations are treated as irrational and the proposed procedures are attempts to avoid adverse effects, such as distortion of the decision-making process. Although allocations are widespread in practice, the complex mathematical procedures developed in the research literature do not appear to be used to any great extent.

The normative tone of the research literature in the 1970s and early 1980s should be apparent from the above discussion. However, the objectives of cost allocations were not well understood. In fact, many researchers regarded allocations as quite unnecessary. It may seem rather strange for a strongly normative literature to lack a clear objective. Nevertheless, the decision-usefulness approach of management accounting's conventional wisdom was clearly visible in this literature and it provided the research objective of deriving allocation procedures to reinforce, or at least not distort, the management decision-making process. As the illustrations used above demonstrate, the decisions were concerned principally with the efficient use of resources and the optimum resource and product mix. As we will see in the next chapter, the recent focus on allocation models has arisen from particular concerns with the management of increasing overhead costs and the determination of product costs for cost control and pricing decisions. These concerns have provided a much clearer objective for cost allocation research and practice.

Activity-Based Costing 12

In Chapter 11 we looked at some of the ways in which common costs can be attributed to production departments. In practice, the direct costs of production departments, together with these attributed common costs, are allocated to individual products using some measure of volume, frequently based on direct labour. Such allocations are needed for, amongst other things, inventory valuations, especially in the financial accounts. But it is argued by writers such as Cooper and Kaplan (eg., 1988) that they also have an impact on management decisions. Indeed, it is the impact of such allocations which led to the claims, mentioned in Chapter 3, that management accounting information is not relevant to the needs of managers in the modern production environment. In this chapter we will look at some of the issues concerning the relevance of accounting information and explore the nature of a proposed alternative which is currently receiving much attention in the professional literature – activity-based costing. We will focus largely on the role of activity-based costing in the determination of product costs. But as will be discussed below, activity-based costing is a response to a wider set of issues.

12.1 The Modern Production Environment

In recent years there have been considerable advances in manufacturing technology with the development of automation, computer–controlled machines, robotics, etc. In many cases, these developments have been essential to cope with increasingly competitive world markets – markets which have become dominated by Japan and other Pacific-rim countries. As illustrated in Figure 12.1 the use of advanced manufacturing technology (AMT) can significantly change the structure of the costs of production – with very large changes in the relative proportions of direct materials, direct labour, inventory holding costs, and the costs of technology (for instance, the costs associated with using and maintaining machinery) in the total costs of production. As production processes become more automated and computer-controlled the costs

FIGURE 12.1
Relationship Between Costs and Increasing Technology

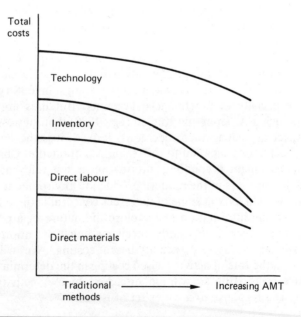

associated with technology increase, but the costs of direct labour fall quite considerably. Hence, there is a dramatic increase in the ratio of overheads to direct labour. It may also be observed that the cost of direct materials declines, but only slightly. This is due to improved use of materials and to the elimination of scrap and waste. It should be noted, however, that the costs associated with inventory holding decline very significantly and may actually tend towards zero. This occurs as companies implement concepts (such as Just-In-Time) aimed at eliminating all forms of waste in the production process.

The traditional approach to inventory management has been to maintain inventories of both raw materials and finished goods, and also buffer stocks between the various stages of the production process, in order to isolate production from the uncertainties of supply and demand. According to management accounting's conventional wisdom the optimal quantities of such inventories should be determined using appropriate mathematical formulae, such as the economic order quantity (EOQ) formula. However, it can be argued that as inventory does not add value to the final product it should be reduced to an absolute minimum. This is one element of a new Japanese management philosophy known as Just-In-Time (JIT), one consequence of which is that manufacturers receive deliveries of raw materials from their suppliers just as they are needed for production. Minimising inventories in this way requires production to be very responsive to the demands of customers. JIT achieves such a responsive production process through the reorganisation of work flows, the use of sophisticated information processing and the introduction of computer-controlled manufacturing systems. In the extreme, such a production process will comprise computer-integrated manufacturing (CIM) and robotics. In such processes the costs of technology will be very high, but with little or no direct labour. In some companies, for example Hewlett Packard (Hunt *et al.*, 1985), direct labour is now treated as an overhead.

Computer-controlled production processes can be very flexible, with the computer determining machine loading, product mix, work scheduling, etc. However, this means that the various parts of the production process are highly integrated and consequently the traditional responsibility centres can become very interdependent. Thus, systems of responsibility accounting with direct production costs attributable to particular cost centres and with the allocation of overheads based on a simple measure of volume are unlikely to provide relevant management information. In modern production environments, overheads are likely to be affected by a wide range of factors: the complexity of the products, the number and size of batches, the quality of output, and so on. Against such a background, the debate concerning the relevance of management accounting information has focused on four specific areas: product costing, overhead management, investment appraisal, and performance evaluation. We will consider each of these in turn.

Product Costing

Traditional systems of product costing were designed for relatively simple, routine manufacturing processes, usually with high labour content. Consequently, overhead allocations tended to be based on either direct labour hours or direct labour costs. These systems appeared to provide satisfactory information for managers in traditional manufacturing industries. But now, with new manufacturing technologies, the labour content is declining rapidly. As a consequence, product costings based on traditional systems involve very high overhead allocation rates. For example, overheads can be as much as 500 per cent of direct labour.

Overhead Management

Changes in the direct labour content of production processes can create considerable distortion in the expected levels of overheads when overhead budgets are set by reference to such ratios. A small change in direct labour in a particular period can lead to a much larger change in the expected overhead. It is argued that such variations make the control of overhead costs very difficult. When overhead budgets are set as a ratio of direct labour there is no real attempt to determine the level of overhead expenditure needed on the individual activities which support the production process. Writers such as Miller and Vollmann (1985) have identified a tendency for 'overhead creep', especially with new technology. This arises because small changes in labour content can create a substantial change in the expected overhead and once these overheads have been incurred they become incorporated into budgets for subsequent periods.

Investment Appraisal

It has been argued that existing accounting techniques can hinder the introduction of new technology (Primrose, 1988). For example, it can be very difficult to quantify costs savings and, more particularly, other intangible long-term benefits of introducing new manufacturing processes. Furthermore, it is almost impossible to quantify the particular risks associated with investments in new technology. This makes it very difficult to apply conventional techniques such as net present value analysis, or even payback. Traditional accounting systems merely allocate technology costs to production processes; no attempts are made to measure its effectiveness.

Performance Evaluation

As advances in technology are changing the nature of production processes, it is becoming increasingly difficult to isolate individual responsibilities and cost pools are tending to become much larger. Consequently, traditional responsibility centres are now far more interdependent than they were in the past and it is necessary to look for alternative ways of evaluating individual contributions to the production process, including non-quantitative factors, such as quality, innovation and meeting work schedules.

12.2 Activity-Based Costing

One proposal for addressing at least some of these problems is to introduce systems of activity-based costing. Such systems relate overhead costs to the various activities which support the production process, as will be described below. Systems of activity-based costing are increasingly being marketed by management consultants in both the US and the UK. These consultants argue that

Western companies are not competitive with their Japanese rivals because management accounting systems in the West are failing to provide the information needed to secure a competitive advantage. Their conclusion is that it is necessary to change existing accounting methods. Such arguments, however, beg some basic questions. Are management accounting systems aimed largely at providing the information needed to secure competitive advantage? What has determined current management accounting practice? Clearly, it is not the provision of information for competitive advantage. Will attempts to change management accounting systems affect other uses of accounting information? We will return to these questions later. Before describing the nature of activity-based costing it is interesting to note that such systems are not used in Japan. But they are 'sold' by management consultants in the West as the solution to the problem of competing with Japanese manufacturers.

As discussed in earlier sections of this book, the conventional wisdom of management accounting is to avoid 'arbitrary' allocations. In Chapter 11 we discussed methods of allocating costs in such a way as to avoid the distortions which would be created by arbitrary allocations. Activity-based costing is a further development in this line of reasoning, and a refinement of the conventional wisdom. Cooper and Kaplan argue that:

> **the theory behind [their] method is simple. Virtually all of a company's activities exist to support the production and delivery of today's goods and services. They should therefore all be considered product costs. And since nearly all factories and corporate support costs are divisible or separable, they can be split apart and traced to individual products or product families. . . . many important cost categories vary not with short-term changes in output but with changes over a period of years in the design, mix, and range of a company's products and customers.** (1988, pp. 96–7)

Activity-based costing moves away from the notions of *short-term* fixed and variable costs which are an important feature of management accounting's conventional wisdom, and focuses on the variability of costs in the longer term. Advocates of activity-based costing claim that all costs are ultimately variable and can be traced to individual products or product lines – including the so-called common costs and costs conventionally regarded as indirect and fixed in the short term. Thus, they argue, it is possible to compute accurate costs for decision making. As we saw in Chapter 11, over the years researchers have been searching for cost allocations which do not distort decision making processes. With activity-based costing some researchers believe they have found a method of providing accurate cost information. Their approach to management decision making, however, is based largely on the simple economic analysis which underlies management accounting's conventional wisdom.

Figure 12.2 illustrates the conventional allocation of common costs in the form of a two-stage process (see Innes and Mitchell,

FIGURE 12.2
Conventional Allocation of Common Costs

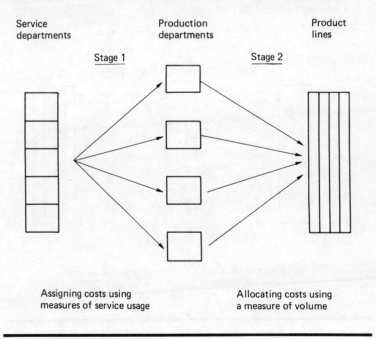

Service departments

Production departments

Product lines

Stage 1

Stage 2

Assigning costs using measures of service usage

Allocating costs using a measure of volume

1990). The first stage involves measuring the various categories of common cost and assigning them to individual production departments using appropriate bases – such as those set out in Table 11.5. Cooper and Kaplan (1988) accept that many companies do this stage very well. It is the next stage which they criticise. This involves allocating these assigned costs to individual product lines using a measure of production volume such as direct labour hours, direct labour costs or machine hours. Cooper and Kaplan claim that such allocations are far too simplistic.

In Figure 12.3 we see an illustration of the activity-based costing approach (see Innes and Mitchell, 1990). This also comprises a

FIGURE 12.3
Activity-Based Costing

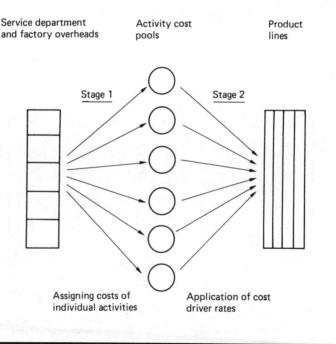

two-stage process. The first stage involves identifying the costs of individual activities and assigning them to activity cost pools. The relevant cost pools will be determined by examining the various activities which support the production and delivery of products. They will include such activities as the setting up of machines, the ordering of raw materials, the supervision of work processes, the despatch of finished goods, and so on. These activities are the 'cost drivers' which give rise to overhead costs. An analysis of cost drivers will determine the appropriate rates to be used in attributing overhead costs to individual products and product lines. In general, the activity cost pools will be constructed in such a way as to facilitate the use of these cost driver rates in the second stage shown in Figure 12.3. This process will be described in the following illustration which uses an approach similar to that taken by Drury (1989).

12.3 An Illustration

Table 12.1 gives various data for a particular period in the life of a hypothetical company. The company has two departments, X and Y, and each department produces two products – department X produces A and B, and department Y produces C and D. Data concerning the sales revenue, direct materials, direct labour, factory overheads and service department costs, including the costs of the selling department, are set out in the table.

Table 12.2 gives a simple computation of product costs. The direct material and direct labour costs for each of the four products are calculated by dividing the total costs in Table 12.1 by the units produced and sold. In this simple computation a blanket rate is used for allocating factory overheads and service department costs. However, as usually suggested in textbooks, the selling expenses are dealt with separately. The total of factory overheads and service department costs are £34 410. This rounds to exactly 400 per cent of the total direct labour cost of £8 600 (£4 600 in department X and £4 000 in department Y). Thus, overheads can be allocated to the individual products using a rate of 400 per cent of direct labour cost. The relevant figures are shown in Table 12.2.

TABLE 12.1
Data for Illustration

	Department X			Department Y		
Products	A	B	Total	C	D	Total
Units produced and sold	1 000	800		1 000	500	
Selling price	£27.50	£30.00		£30.00	£35.00	
Sales revenue	£27 500	£24 000	£51 500	£30 000	£17 500	£47 500
Costs incurred:						
direct materials	10 000	6 400	16 400	9 000	7 500	16 500
direct labour	3 000	1 600	4 600	3 000	1 000	4 000
			£21 000			£20 500

Factory overheads:	
set-up	£ 1 370
supervision	2 400
machines	19 800
	£23 570

Service department costs:	
purchasing	£ 4 440
warehouse and despatch	3 100
power	3 300
	£10 840

Selling expenses	£ 7 920

TABLE 12.2
Simple Computation of Product Costs

	Products			
	A	B	C	D
	£	£	£	£
Direct materials	10.00	8.00	9.00	15.00
Direct labour	3.00	2.00	3.00	2.00
400% of direct labour	12.00	8.00	12.00	8.00
Product cost	25.00	18.00	24.00	25.00
Selling expenses (8% of selling prices)	2.20	2.40	2.40	2.80
Total cost	27.20	20.40	26.40	27.80
Selling price	27.50	30.00	30.00	35.00
Profit	0.30	9.60	3.60	7.20

Overheads:
	£
factory	23,570
service department	10,840
	£34,410 =

To compute the total cost of each product we must add the selling expenses. As the selling expenses amount to £7 920, or 8 per cent of the total sales revenue of £99 000 (£51 500 in department X and £47 500 in department Y), they can be allocated to each product at 8 per cent of its selling price, as shown in Table 12.2. The resulting total costs can then be used to compute the profit for each of the four products. Having computed these product profitabilities management might wish to consider its marketing strategy. But before discussing such a strategy it will be helpful for us to look at the nature of the four products.

Product A is a standard product which is produced for one customer, according to the requirements of a long-term contract. Products B and C are produced largely in response to orders received from a small number of customers, but limited numbers are produced for inventory. Product D is produced in a range of different colours and is usually produced for stock, with orders being dispatched from the warehouse as required. All four products are very similar and at present the company believes that the basic price for all four should be in the region of £30. However, product A is sold at a discount of £2.50 which was negotiated in connection with the long-term contract, and a premium of £5 is charged for Product D because it is available on demand from inventory in a range of different colours. Looking at the relative profitabilities in Table 12.2, it might be concluded that product A is not very attractive as it is only just breaking even. The company might want to reconsider its commitment to the long-term contract. Products B and D look the most profitable; possibly production should be directed towards these products.

Such simple calculations of product costs could be misleading as far as the relative profitabilities of the four products are concerned. Maybe a more sophisticated analysis of the products is needed. Tables 12.3 and 12.4 illustrate the calculation of product costs using the methods of allocating common costs which were described in Chapter 11. The first stage, as shown in Table 12.3, is to assign the common costs to the production departments. The factory overheads which comprise set up, supervision, and machine costs can be measured separately in the two production departments. Thus, there is no need for an allocation base at this stage.

TABLE 12.3
Allocating of Common Costs

	Total	Production departments	
		X	Y
	£	£	£
Factory overheads:			
Set up	1 370	470	900
Supervision	2 400	1 200	1 200
Machines	19 800	10 800	9 000
Allocation of common costs:			
Purchasing department (material costs)	4 440	2 213	2 227
Warehouse and despatch (units produced)	3 100	1 691	1 409
Power plant (machine hours worked)	3 300	1 800	1 500
		£18 174	£16 236
Machine hour rate		£20.20	£21.64

But for the service department costs some basis of allocation is needed. It is decided that the purchasing department's costs should be allocated to the two production departments on the basis of their relative direct material costs. Direct materials are £16 400 in department X and £16 500 in department Y. The purchasing department's costs of £4 440 are allocated in these proportions. In the case of the warehouse and despatch department, it is decided that the number of units produced in the two departments provide an acceptable allocation basis. Thus, the units produced in department X, 1800, and the units produced in department Y, 1500, provide the basis for allocating the warehouse and despatch department's costs of £3100. Finally, as the power plant is used exclusively to provide the power for the machinery used in department X and department Y, and as the machines are similar in both departments, the machine hours worked in the two departments are to be used as the basis of allocation. Each product requires one-half hour of machine time, and during the period the machines are used for 1650 hours – 900 hours in department X and 750 hours in department Y. This gives the ratio for allocating the power plant's costs of £3300. As can be seen in Table 12.3, the total common costs allocated to the two departments are £18174 to department X and £16236 to department Y.

The second stage in the computation of product costs is to allocate these common costs to the individual products on the basis of some measure of production volume, as shown in Table 12.4. For purposes of our illustration, this allocation is based on the machine hours worked. Using the machine hours of 900 in department X and 750 in department Y we can compute machine hour rates for the two departments – £20.20 in department X and £21.64 in department Y, as shown in Table 12.3. In each case we have divided the total costs of the department by its machine hour usage. In principle it would be possible to allocate the various elements of these total costs using different allocation bases. For instance, the purchasing department's costs could be allocated on the basis of the direct materials in each product. However, the use of a single rate, such as a machine hour rate, seems to be the most common in practice.

Table 12.4 illustrates the calculation of the individual product costs. Direct materials and direct labour are the same as in Table 12.2. The factory overheads and allocated common costs are based on the machine hour rates computed in Table 12.3. Remember each product requires one-half hour of machine time. Finally, the selling expenses are allocated at the rate of 8 per cent of selling prices, as in Table 12.2.

If we now look at the relative profitabilities of the four products, it appears that product A is profitable. But product B is by far the most profitable, with products C and D both more profitable than

TABLE 12.4
Common Cost Allocation: Computing Product Costs

	Products			
	A £	B £	C £	D £
Direct materials	10.00	8.00	9.00	15.00
Direct labour	3.00	2.00	3.00	2.00
Factory overheads and allocated common costs (using machine hour rate)	10.10	10.10	10.82	10.82
Production cost	23.10	20.10	22.82	27.82
Selling expenses (8% of selling price)	2.20	2.40	2.40	2.80
Total cost	25.30	22.50	25.22	30.62
Selling price	27.50	30.00	30.00	35.00
Profit	2.20	7.50	4.78	4.38

product A. The management may still wish to consider the relative attractiveness of the long-term contract, but they may be prepared to accept this somewhat lower profitability given the assured demand which the contract provides. However, the advocates of activity-based costing would argue that such figures may be unreliable indicators of product profitability, as the arbitrary allocations, especially the blanket machine hour rate, can give rise to misleading product costs. They would suggest that we identify the activity cost drivers and construct appropriate activity cost pools.

12.4 Activity-Based Costing in Action

To identify activity cost drivers we need to consider, for each element of cost, how the relevant activities support the productive process. Consider first the various elements of factory overheads. The machines are obviously the central element of the productive process. The set up involves preparing the relevant machines for each batch of a particular product. The supervision provides support to the individual machine operatives by giving advice, ensuring continuity of supplies, and taking decisions on various production-related matters. For each of these costs it is probably appropriate to create a separate activity cost pool.

Now turning to the service departments. An analysis of the activities of the purchasing department indicates that there are two distinct activities, order processing and materials handling. Order processing comprises the clerical work associated with obtaining supplies of raw materials, whereas materials handling involves the physical handling of those raw materials when they are received. A similar analysis of the warehouse and despatch department indicates that, once again, there are two distinct activities; the storage of finished goods and the despatch of orders to customers. In the case of the power plant, as already discussed, all the expense relates to the single activity of providing power for the machinery. Finally, the selling expenses are concerned with the single activity of obtaining orders for the company's products. An analysis of the various costs yields the amounts in each of the activity cost pools shown in Table 12.5. If an activity-based costing system is introduced these costs should be measured directly by the accounting system.

This completes the first stage of Figure 12.3. The next stage involves the application of these activity costs to the individual products using appropriate cost drivers. We will discuss each of these activity cost pools in turn. Using the additional data set out in Table 12.6 we can compute the activity-based product costs shown in Table 12.7.

TABLE 12.5
Activity Cost Pools

Activity	£
Set up	1 370
Supervision	2 400
Machines	19 800
Order processing	440
Materials handling	4 000
Finished goods storage	1 600
Despatch	1 500
Power	3 300
Selling	7 920

TABLE 12.6
Data for Cost Drivers

	Products			
Cost drivers	A	B	C	D
Production batch size (units)	100	50	100	25
Set up time (hours)	1.5	2	1	4
Supervisors' time per period (hours)	75	40	75	50
Machine time per unit (hour)	0.5	0.5	0.5	0.5
Orders processed per period	10	20	20	60
Raw material inputs per unit	2	5	2	4
Average holding of finished goods (units)	0	100	100	200
Number of deliveries per period	10	40	50	200
Sales staff time per period (hours)	32	160	200	400

Set up £1 370:   Table 12.6 indicates the batch size for each of the four products, together with the set up time required prior to each production run. Dividing the total production for each of the four products shown in Table 12.1 by these batch sizes indicates that during the period we have 10 production runs for product A, 16 for product B, 10 for product C and 20 for product D. If we now multiply these production runs by the set up time per run, we can calculate the total set up time during the period: 15 hours, 32 hours, 10 hours and 80 hours respectively for the four products, a total of 137 hours. As the total cost for set up is £1 370, the cost per set up hour is £10. Using this cost we can compute the set up cost component of the product costs. For instance, as product A requires 1.5 hours set up, this will entail a cost of £15 for a production run of 100 units – a cost per unit of £0.15. For product B the set up cost will be £20 for a production run of 50 – a unit set up cost of £0.40. And so on.

Supervision £2 400:   An analysis has been undertaken of the time spent by the individual supervisors on the four products. This indicates that the time spent during the current period (a typical period) was 75 hours for product A, 40 hours for product B, 75 hours for product C and 50 hours for product D (as shown in Table 12.6): a total of 240 hours. This gives a cost per hour for supervision of £10. The time spent on each of the products can now be used to compute the individual product costs. For product A, 75 hours of supervision is required, costing £750 for production of 1 000 units: a unit cost of £0.75. For product B, 40 hours is required, costing £400 for production of 800 units: a unit cost of £0.50. Similar calculations can be made for products C and D.

Machines £19 800:   As already indicated, the machine time per hour is the same for each product, i.e., 0.5 hours. Using this time in conjunction with the output for the current period (1 000 product A, 800 product B, 1 000 product C and 500 product D), we can calculate that the total machine time is 1 650 hours. Dividing the cost of the machines, £19 800, by this total time gives a cost of £12 per hour. Thus, the cost per unit produced is £6 (for half an hour) for all four products.

Order processing £440: Table 12.6 sets out the number of orders processed for each of the four products. In total, 110 orders were processed at a cost of £440; a cost per order of £4. Thus, in the case of product A the processing cost for the period was £40 (10 orders at £4 per order). As this is for a production of 1000 units, the cost per unit is £0.04. Similar calculations can be made for products B, C and D.

Materials handling £4000: The raw material inputs for each product are shown in Table 12.6. Applying these to the production for the current period, we calculate that the total raw material inputs were 2000 for product A, 4000 for product B, 2000 for product C and 2000 for product D: a total of 10000 raw material inputs. As the cost of materials handling is £4000, the cost per unit of raw material handled is £0.40. This cost can be applied to the raw material input per unit in Table 12.6 to calculate the material handling cost per unit.

Finished goods storage £1600: Table 12.6 shows the average holding of finished goods for the four products. Remember, product A is produced only for one customer and delivery takes place immediately production is completed. Therefore, there is no inventory of product A. But there are inventories of products B, C and D – on average, 100, 100 and 200 units respectively. As the four products are very similar, it is estimated that the inventory holding costs will be the same for each of the four products. Thus, the average holding of, in total, 400 units at a cost of £1600 gives a cost per unit of inventory of £4. Thus, the finished goods storage cost for product B is £400 and, as the current production is 800 units, the finished goods storage cost per unit of product B is £0.50. Similar calculations can be made for products C and D.

Despatch £1500: The number of deliveries per period for each of the four products are shown in Table 12.6, from which it can be calculated that the total deliveries during the period were 300, at a cost of £1500; giving a cost per delivery of £5. Thus, as the delivery cost for product A for the period was £50, for sales of 1000 units, the unit cost is £0.05. Again, similar calculations can be made for the other three products.

Power £3 300:   As indicated earlier, power is required for the production machines and consequently it is appropriate to apply the costs of power on the basis of the machine hours worked. As calculated above, 1 650 machine hours were worked during the period. With the costs of power amounting to £3 300 this gives a cost per machine hour of £2. Thus, as each product requires half a machine hour, the cost per product is £1.

Selling £7 920:   A detailed analysis has been undertaken of the time spent by members of the sales staff on each of the four products – these are shown in Table 12.6. Little time is required for product A as sales of this product are derived from the long-term contract. Most effort is required for the sales of product D. There are a large number of customers for this product and it is carried in a variety of different colours. Total sales staff time for the current period amounts to 792 hours and, as the cost of the selling department was £7 920, the cost per hour is £10. Thus, in the case of A, the total selling cost for the period is £320 (32 hours at £10 per hour). With sales of 1 000 units, this represents a product cost of £0.32. Similar calculations can be made for the other three products.

These calculations provide the elements of the product costs set out in Table 12.7. If these costs are subtracted from the selling prices of the four products, we can compute their relative profitabilities. It can now be seen that products A, B and C are all quite profitable, while product D incurs a substantial loss. This is a very different picture from that set out in Tables 12.2 and 12.4. To compare the various figures, the information concerning product costs and profitability are summarised in Table 12.8, where we see a significant variation in the unit costs and, in particular, in the relative profitabilities of the four products.

Activity-based costing shows product D to have a negative margin, whereas the other two methods showed it to be profitable. This is because product D is more complex (because of the number of variants produced and the smaller batch size), has a larger inventory, and requires more time from the sales staff. But in the simple costing calculations, even when the conventional allocation of common costs was used, the costs of complexity, inventory and

TABLE 12.7
Activity-Based Costing: Computing Product Costs

| | Products | | | |
	A £	B £	C £	D £
Direct materials	10.00	8.00	9.00	15.00
Direct labour	3.00	2.00	3.00	2.00
Set up	0.15	0.40	0.10	1.60
Supervision	0.75	0.50	0.75	1.00
Machines	6.00	6.00	6.00	6.00
Order processing	0.04	0.10	0.08	0.48
Materials handling	0.80	2.00	0.80	1.60
Finished goods storage	0.00	0.50	0.40	1.60
Despatch	0.05	0.25	0.25	2.00
Power	1.00	1.00	1.00	1.00
Selling expenses	0.32	2.00	2.00	8.00
Total cost	22.11	22.75	23.38	40.28
Selling price	27.50	30.00	30.00	35.00
Profit	5.39	7.25	6.62	−5.28

TABLE 12.8
Comparison of Costing Systems

	Products A £	B £	C £	D £
Cost per unit:				
Simple costing	27.20	20.40	26.40	27.80
Allocation of common costs	25.30	22.50	25.22	30.62
Activity-based costing	22.11	22.75	23.38	40.28
Selling price	27.50	30.00	30.00	35.00
Profitability per unit:				
Simple costing	0.30	9.60	3.60	7.20
margin %	1%	32%	12%	21%
Allocation of common costs	2.20	7.50	4.78	4.38
margin %	8%	25%	16%	13%
Activity-based costing	5.39	7.25	6.62	−5.28
margin %	20%	24%	22%	Negative

selling were not separately identified for the individual products. Rather they were subsumed in the overhead costs which were spread more or less evenly across the products. Activity-based costing attempts to measure the costs of the underlying activities which support the production and delivery of the individual products. Advocates of activity-based costing argue that managers using simple costing or a method in which common costs are allocated to production departments could make incorrect decisions if they relied on such product cost information. For instance, in our illustration the costing calculations which rely on simple measures of volume to allocate overhead costs could lead managers to believe that the price of product A should be increased or its production discontinued (if this is possible within the terms of the contract), as it is only just breaking even. However, activity-based costing demonstrates that Product A is almost as profitable as products B and C, and it is product D which should be discontinued if its price cannot be increased or its costs reduced.

12.5 Potential and Limitations

The above illustration has demonstrated the nature and usefulness of activity-based costing in the calculation of product costs. As we saw, activity-based costing traces to individual products the costs of the activities which give rise to overhead expenditure. In theory, it should be possible to trace all overheads, but in practice it is quite likely that there will be some costs which cannot be traced to individual products (e.g., the costs of the head office administrative staff) and some arbitrary allocations may remain. But the objective of activity-based costing is to reduce such allocations to a minimum. In this way, managers should receive better information about their product costs.

Traditional methods of allocation average overhead costs across all products. This leads to cross-subsidisation and possibly to incorrect decisions being made. For example, products which are complex, difficult to manufacture, and produced to special order are subsidised by the simple, large batch products. With traditional accounting systems the former products are allocated overheads at the same average rate as the latter, although they require far greater support and consequently higher overhead expenditure. As we saw in the illustration, the simple allocation methods could have encouraged managers to drop product A and to focus on product D. Activity-based costing, however, gives a much clearer indication of the relative costs of such products and should lead to better decision making.

In highlighting the usefulness of activity-based costing in the calculation of product costs, we must not overlook its other potential contributions. The focus on activities and the periodic reporting of cost drivers draw management attention to the factors which give rise to overhead expenditure. Knowledge of cost drivers should improve the planning and management of overhead costs. For example, the traditional view of overheads as a percentage of labour costs could encourage budgeting practices in which appropriations for overheads are based on a predetermined direct labour rate, rather than an analysis of the activities required to support the production planned for the period. Such an analysis would identify the expenditure needed to support the budgeted production. In the above illustration, for instance, knowledge of cost driver rates for order processing and materials handling could be used to determine a budget for the purchasing department which would be linked directly to the planned production of the four products. Such overhead budgets are likely to lead to improved management and control of overheads.

As mentioned earlier, with existing accounting methods it can be very difficult to evaluate investment in new technology. Activity-based costing, however, can provide relevant information concerning the costs of the existing technology and this can be used as a starting point for assessing the potential costs and benefits of technological developments. In addition, an analysis of cost drivers will provide a wide range of performance measures with which to assess the activities of both production and service departments. For instance, the monitoring of inventory holding costs and the costs per delivery of the four products will provide relevant performance measures for the warehouse and despatch department in the illustration.

An important element of activity-based costing and cost driver analysis which has not been mentioned so far is the identification and elimination of non-value-added items. As mentioned earlier, cost driver analysis involves identifying the various activities which support the production and delivery of products. This support can be assessed in terms of the value added to the final product. However, if there are activities within the business which do not add value to the final products they represent a drain on the resources and should be eliminated. In analysing cost drivers attempts can be made to identify non-value-added activities and to look for ways in which they can be eliminated. Thus, activity-based costing reinforces the JIT philosophy of reducing all forms of waste.

Returning to the role of activity-based costing in the calculation of product costs, it is claimed by the authors of articles on the subject that activity-based costing can lead to more accurate product costs than the more conventional methods of management accounting. These authors have, in general, been careful to avoid notions of 'true' product costs. Nevertheless, the way in which activity-based costing is advocated does imply that it has the potential to provide the 'correct' information for managers. Thus, there are similarities with the 'absolute truth' approach which we discussed earlier in connection with the era of cost accounting. In some ways, the arguments surrounding activity-based costing are similar to those used in discussions about product costing over fifty years ago.

As discussed in the earlier sections of this book, since the era of absolute truth in cost accounting many new ideas have been advanced, for example different costs for different purposes, the role of risk and uncertainty, and the importance of understanding information costs and benefits. Initially, activity-based costing tended to be over-sold by some of its more enthusiastic advocates. However, it now seems to be accepted that activity-based costing is not necessarily appropriate for all businesses. In some cases, especially where a simple product mix is produced, it may be appropriate to use more traditional methods of cost allocation. In addition, where activity-based costing is used, it may be necessary to modify cost drivers from time to time, especially as the focus of corporate objectives shifts. Furthermore, modifications may also be necessary as new product lines are introduced or new technological developments implemented. In addition, it is now accepted that it is not essential to apply activity-based costing to all costs, or to the entire accounting system. Activity-based costing can be used alongside a more traditional cost accounting system.

12.6 When to Use Activity-Based Costing

In discussing the question 'Does your company need a new cost system?', Cooper (1987) suggested that managers should ask themselves 'Do I really know what my products cost?'. If the answer to this question is 'no', he argued that managers should consider whether it is necessary to undertake a detailed analysis of their cost accounting system. But rather than undertaking a major and costly analysis in every case, he suggested that managers look for the following symptoms which are indicative of a need for activity-based costing:

(i) Products that are very difficult to produce are reported to be very profitable, even though they are not premium-priced. As we saw in the illustration, although product D was more difficult to produce than other products, its costs were apparently no higher, when we used conventional cost allocation procedures. Cooper argues that products which are difficult to produce should be expected to cost more and, therefore, to be profitable only if they are priced at a premium.

(ii) Profit margins cannot be easily explained. If managers believe certain products to be more profitable than the accounting systems suggest, it may be necessary to analyse costs using activity-based costing.

(iii) Some products not sold by competitors have high reported margins. Competitors would normally be expected to produce products which are very profitable. Why are they not producing these products? They may consider the costs to be too high.

(iv) The results of bids or tenders are difficult to explain. A company which regularly submits bids for contracts or tenders for work and finds that its low prices are rejected and/or its high prices accepted may need to examine its cost system. Its perceptions of low and high prices might not be shared by competitors and customers.

(v) Competitors' high volume products are priced at apparently unrealistically low levels. If competitors are able to price their products at levels which appear unrealistically low, it may be that the firm's costing system needs examining.

(vi) Suppliers offer to produce parts at prices considerably lower than expected. Managers considering buying in parts currently produced internally who find that suppliers offer them at unexpectedly low prices should examine their costing systems.

(vii) Cost pools are too large and contain machines that have very different overhead structures. This creates considerable complexity and could mean that the procedures for allocating the overheads will be too simplistic.

(viii) The cost of marketing and delivering products varies dramatically by distribution channel, and yet the cost accounting system effectively ignores marketing costs. The earlier illustration contained a good example.

Managers should look for these symptoms and ask themselves whether they have confidence in their product cost information. As the symptoms may have other explanations, it is important to consider the range of possibilities and to evaluate which is the more likely. However, even if it appears that existing product costs are misleading it may not always be necessary to incorporate activity-based costing into the accounting system. It must be remembered that the introduction of an activity-based costing system involves major expense and thus managers must ask themselves whether the benefits to be derived from the superior information exceed the costs of the new accounting system.

In the illustration, product costs were first calculated using traditional methods of allocation and then activity-based costing was introduced. Various analyses were undertaken to identify activities and the associated cost drivers. If activity-based costing is to be used in future periods two possibilities are available:

(1) Integrate activity-based costing into the accounting system, so that all routine accounting reports contain activity-based costs.
(2) Leave the accounting system unchanged and analyse costs using an activity-based approach as the need arises for such information, e.g., when pricing new products or making product mix decisions.

The choice between these two possibilities should be based on their respective costs and benefits, and a consideration of the role of accounting information in the management of the business.

12.7 The Future of Activity-Based Costing

Earlier in this chapter it was pointed out that some of the arguments advanced for activity-based costing beg some basic questions, including 'are management accounting systems aimed largely at providing information needed to secure competitive advantage?'. It might be argued, for example, that traditional accounting systems are designed with stewardship in mind to keep track of expenditures incurred, and not to provide the forward- and outward-looking information needed to secure competitive advantage. Such information may be provided from other sources. For instance, it was suggested in Chapter 3 that price setters may, in practice, modify the information they receive from accounting systems to take account of competitive factors. Furthermore, the prices of most products are determined by supply and demand in the market place, and cost information is only of secondary importance. In such circumstances decision makers need information from outside the business, such as customers' preferences, competitors' costs and so on.

Much of the research for activity-based costing and many of the case studies which have been published are based in US defence-related industries where prices are largely cost determined. In such industries regular product cost information is important. But the role of product costs is not so clear in other industries, especially service industries, and it is possible that satisfactory product cost information can be obtained in other ways.

However, it is important to distinguish cost management from product costing. Even if product costing is not of primary importance, activity-based costing may still have a major role to play in cost management. The focus on activities and cost drivers provides a basis for monitoring the costs of both production and service departments. As advances in technology change patterns of cost behaviour, activity-based costing forces accountants (and managers) to understand the new production processes, and directs cost control to the source of overhead costs (the activities), rather than their consequences (the production). In the future, we are likely to see activity-based cost control playing an important role in many businesses.

But it is important to recognise that activity-based costing is not a panacea. It is not *the* answer to the lack of competitiveness of Western industry. Certainly it has a contribution to make. It will help managers focus on activities and cost drivers in an era of new technology. But it is not clear that activity-based costing will necessarily lead to greater profits in all companies. Admittedly, there are case studies of companies in which activity-based costing has improved profitability, but only the future will tell whether other companies will find activity-based costing equally successful.

Some Possible Future Developments 13

In the first section of this book (Chapters 1, 2 and 3) it was suggested that there is an apparent gap between the theory and practice of management accounting. At least two approaches are available to anyone who wishes to explore this apparent gap. The first approach would entail investigating the practice of management accounting, while the alternative would involve reappraising the theory. The latter approach has been adopted in this book. The so-called theory of management accounting has been reappraised through a review of contemporary developments in the research literature.

As the starting point for this review, theory was equated with the conventional wisdom of management accounting, as portrayed in current textbooks. It was argued in Chapter 2 that the contents of such textbooks are the result of research undertaken primarily in the 1960s. The term 'conditional truth' was used to depict the general theme of this research and to distinguish it from the 'absolute truth' theme of the earlier cost accounting literature. The notion of 'conditional truth' is appropriate because different costs are needed for different purposes or, in other words, because accounting information can be determined only in relation to users' information needs.

In developing management accounting concepts and techniques researchers had to identify managers' information needs. This meant constructing decision models to indicate how decisions should be made. Once a decision model is postulated, the notion of conditional truth implies that the appropriate information can be determined by deductive reasoning. An economic framework played a central role in structuring the decision models used by management accounting researchers. In that framework the decision maker was assumed to have available, at no cost and with no uncertainty, all the information needed to completely structure any decision problem and to arrive at a profit maximising solution. Decision makers were presumed to possess the necessary knowledge required to use any of the techniques developed by researchers and costless information processing placed no limits on the complexity of the information system. It was assumed that once a decision was analysed, the appropriate accounting information could be determined.

The research reviewed in later sections of the book attempted to relax some of the assumptions of these decision models. The first step was to relax the assumption concerning certainty. This led to a variety of complex decision models, such as the cost–volume–profit and cost variance investigation models discussed in Chapters 5 and 6. However, when uncertainty is introduced into the analysis, questions concerning the cost and value of information become important. Information can reduce uncertainty, but it is a costly resource and, like any other resource, its production should be evaluated in terms of costs and benefits. Developments in the field of information economics described in Chapters 7 and 8 provided researchers with the necessary tools to evaluate information costs and benefits in management accounting contexts. Amongst other things, this research led to the interesting conclusion that the simple techniques which are frequently observed in practice could represent optimal responses to the costs and benefits of information in particular decision situations.

The conclusions reached by information economics researchers led to the change of emphasis in management accounting research which was discussed in Chapter 9 and which has been carried through into the more recent work using agency theory models described in Chapter 10. This change of emphasis involved recognising that researchers should not necessarily criticise practitioners for their limited use of the quantitative approaches proposed in the research literature. As a result the gap between the theory and practice of management accounting came to be viewed from quite a new perspective. From this perspective questions concerning the practical application of the theory, especially the conventional wisdom of management accounting, become the focus of attention. For example, in what circumstances can particular theoretical concepts and techniques be used in practice?

Unfortunately, the theoretical literature lacks generalisable prescriptions and, furthermore, information economics suggests that the value of information is situation specific. Nevertheless, the change of emphasis in management accounting research was an important development as it led to a revised interpretation of the relationship between theory and practice. It suggested a need for researchers to approach the gap (between theory and practice) from the alternative direction – that is, by investigating the nature of management accounting practice.

As described in Chapter 3, researchers are now beginning to study management accounting practice. Some studies have attempted to understand management accounting in wider organisational and social terms than the simple economic model of the conventional wisdom. But other studies are simply attempts to extend the conventional wisdom to encompass recent developments in the competitive nature of world markets and advances in manufacturing technology. The work of Kaplan and his colleagues in the US are illustrations of the latter type of study. Kaplan, in particular, has received considerable attention in the professional press because of his arguments that management accounting has lost its relevance and his description of a crisis in management accounting. We referred to some of his arguments in Chapter 3 and here we will examine further the nature of the supposed crisis.

13.1 Crisis in Management Accounting?

Based on studies in the US, Johnson and Kaplan (1987) argued that management accounting has a major crisis: 'Today's management accounting information, driven by the procedures and cycle of the organization's financial reporting system, is too late, too aggregated, and too distorted to be relevant for managers' planning and control decisions' (p. 1). As was discussed in Chapter 3, they claim that there have been no major developments in management accounting practices in recent years and consequently management accounting is now living off the innovations made sixty, eighty and a hundred years ago.

Johnson and Kaplan's arguments are based on a belief that the demands for financial accounting information have distorted management accounting systems to such an extent that management accounting is now subservient to financial reporting. Consequently, managers are more concerned with the short-term impact of their decisions on stock market prices than with the long-term competitive position and profitability of their businesses. Furthermore, because of the importance attached to the financial reporting cycle, management information is often too aggregated and too late to be of use in operational control. Johnson and Kaplan place some of the blame for this lack of relevance on business schools and academic accountants, because of their focus on simplified decision settings which ignore competitive and technological advances.

Kaplan and other writers associate the failure of Western companies to compete in world markets dominated by the Japanese with this lack of relevance in management accounting, the clear implication being that it is management accountants who are largely to blame. Although routine accounting systems may be determined by the requirements of financial reporting, it is far from clear that all management accounting information comes from these systems. Kaplan may be over-emphasising their importance; relevant information may be available from other sources. The proposed response to this perceived crisis is 'revolutionary' change in accounting systems with the introduction of activity-based costing. Such a response is intended to ensure that management accountants provide all relevant information, and that management decisions are based entirely on accounting numbers. An alternative approach would be to explore ways in which managers can use both accounting and non-accounting information in their decision making.

In a response to Johnson and Kaplan, a report prepared for the Chartered Institute of Management Accountants by Bromwich and Bhimani (1989) called for *Evolution not Revolution*. They reviewed various studies of management accounting practice in the UK and, although they could identify no major changes in systems and techniques, they did observe important changes in the nature of management accounting practice. In particular, they claimed that management accountants are now more integrated into the functional areas of the business. For example, there is increasing use of multi-disciplinary teams, comprising managers and others drawn from the different functional areas who, together with management accountants, tackle particularly complex decision problems. In addition, management accountants are now more directly involved in day-to-day decisions through the provision of informal/non-routine information. There is also increasing recognition of the need for management accounting to be outward-looking (for example, to identify competitors' cost structures as well as the company's own) and to report non-quantitative information (for example, information about quality, innovations, etc.). etc.).

Accordingly, Bromwich and Bhimani did not see a crisis in management accounting; at least not in the terms which Johnson and Kaplan had used in respect of the US. They also did not see a need for revolutionary changes in management accounting systems, although they accepted that activity-based costing could be useful in some companies. Nevertheless, they did make recommendations. These were intended to reinforce the changes in management accounting practice which they had identified. They urged accountants to improve their informal communication with functional managers, and suggested that it is important for accountants to learn the language of operational activities. They recommended that companies improve their flows of non-financial information, such as information about quality, scrap and reject rates, delivery efficiency, machine integrity and so on. They also encouraged accountants to develop systems of strategic management accounting which will evaluate products from the customers' points of view, estimate costs relative to competitors, and generally help long-term planning and the formulation of corporate strategy.

In making these recommendations, Bromwich and Bhimani explicitly recognised the organisational constraints on the development of management accounting. For example, they argued that accounting systems should be designed to fit the organisation and not vice versa. They also emphasised the political nature of organisational processes which means that accounting data may be manipulated, used partially, etc. to justify particular decisions. Consequently, new accounting techniques should not be imposed without considerable thought, and should be evaluated in their organisational context. The danger with unthoughtful introduction of techniques such as activity-based costing is that they may be perceived as attempts by accountants to impose unnecessary controls on functional managers, and thus they may encounter resistance, manipulation of data, and so on. The alternative, which Bromwich and Bhimani seem to be suggesting, is that accountants should increase their understanding of the functional areas and be more sympathetic to the needs of the functional managers. We can explore this issue further by looking at the dual nature of management accounting.

13.2 The Dual Nature of Management Accounting

Consider the accountant of an operating unit in a large multi-divisional company. Such an accountant will probably be regarded as part of the unit's decision-making team. This represents a productive role, through which the accountant assists managers to pursue the unit's objectives. But at the same time, the accountant will also be responsible to head office for financial reports. This represents a control role, in which the accountant acts on behalf of senior managers. These two roles can be contradictory and lead to ambiguity and tension in the accountant's work.

If we want to change accounting practices in order to improve corporate profitability, which of these two roles should receive our attention? On the one hand, the productive role could be facilitated by greater integration of the accountant into functional areas, by improvements in informal information and communication, and by the provision of non-quantitative and strategic information. This seems to be the approach taken by Bromwich and Bhimani. On the other hand, the control role could be facilitated by ensuring that accounting systems 'accurately' reflect the impact of new technology and 'correctly' measure product costs, so that accounting reports are better control devices through which senior managers can monitor the actions of middle managers. This seems to be the approach of Kaplan and others in the US.

An approach which emphasises increased accounting control may be resented by functional managers who could perceive accountants to be increasing their own power in the organisation. How might such managers respond? In a number of the case studies used to promote activity-based costing the companies concerned were already in a financial crisis, and something needed to be done. In these cases, the introduction of activity-based costing was seen as a welcome solution. But in other companies, where there are no immediate crises, it is not clear how managers will respond to such revolutionary change. Possibly a more evolutionary approach may be better received.

As already mentioned, in Japan activity-based costing is not widely used. The limited (and largely anecdotal) evidence which is available suggests that management accounting has a quite limited role in Japanese companies, with accounting information being used to support other information flows; in particular, information about the market. Market prices appear to determine product costs, and not vice versa. There are reports of Japanese managers estimating the prices they believe the market will bear and then managing their production to achieve these prices. Management accounting does not appear to have a major control function. Control seems to be based largely on loyalty, seniority, trust, national culture, etc.

To complete this discussion it is worth quoting a comment made by Spicer (1990) in a review of the Bromwich and Bhimani report:

> **While endless discussion about 'crisis' in management accounting makes for good press it is not a particularly productive debate . . . In my view it is more productive to start by accepting the fact that the competitive environment is changing rapidly and then directly address the questions of how and why firms need to (and are) changing their manufacturing and marketing strategies, organisational forms, and cost and management accounting systems to capture sustainable competitive advantage.**

These questions raise the important point that we still need to know how and why particular management accounting practices are adopted. Despite the case studies published to date, we still have only limited understanding of the factors which influence the nature of management accounting practice. Thus, in order to be able to evaluate the likely consequences of introducing activity-based costing, we need a theoretical framework capable of explaining existing practices. As mentioned earlier, such a framework is not yet available, but following the change of emphasis identified in Chapter 9, researchers now recognise its importance.

13.3 Some Implications of the Change of Emphasis

Until the determinants of existing management accounting practice are better understood it will be extremely hazardous to make generalised statements not only about accounting techniques such as activity-based costing, but also about such techniques as cost–volume–profit analysis, variance investigation models, linear programming, and so on. Such techniques provide a stock of methods which are available to practitioners, i.e., a tool-chest. But little can be said at the theoretical level about the techniques (tools) which should generally be used in practice. For instance, it cannot be said that activity-based costing should always be preferred to other methods of cost allocation.

The conventional wisdom of management accounting does not provide a comprehensive set of techniques which ought to be used in practice. The techniques which comprise the conventional wisdom form a subset of the available alternatives from which practitioners may select; but the extension into activity-based costing and the complex quantitative techniques proposed by researchers in the early 1970s also form part of the available set; as do the techniques developed in allied disciplines. Thus, accounting students (and anybody else studying management accounting) should recognise the range of available alternatives. In evaluating each alternative it is important to identify any implementation problems, both quantitative and behavioural, and to assess the potential costs and benefits in actual applications.

In addition to understanding and developing individual techniques (i.e., the system design issues), consideration should be given to the factors which could be relevant when choosing a management accounting system, such as information costs/benefits, behavioural factors and organisational characteristics (i.e., the elements of the system choice problem). Although unique solutions to such problems are not available, the information economics and agency theory literatures indicate a number of factors which may require consideration. For instance, information economics has emphasised the importance of recognising information costs and benefits, and of separating the system design issues from information system choice problems. In addition, agency theory has demonstrated the need to consider the motivations of managers who may be influenced by accounting systems and, also, the possible effects of information asymmetries. Thus, anyone studying management accounting should keep these factors in mind when exploring the techniques offered in current textbooks.

Ongoing and future theoretical management accounting research may provide a framework for evaluating particular techniques. But for the present, a suitable framework is not available. However, the change of emphasis discussed above represents an important step in that direction. Attempts to explain existing practices should generate insights into the role of management accounting, which will help in the building of theoretical structures for practical research. At present much of the research aimed at developing new techniques, including activity-based costing, can be criticised for its limited theoretical framework. As already pointed out, activity-based costing is an extension of the conventional wisdom. Whereas theoretical advances in areas such as information economics and agency theory seek to explain existing practice, the research into activity-based costing is largely dismissive of existing practice. Johnson and Kaplan do attempt a theoretical explanation of management accounting's lack of relevance, but their arguments are expressed in terms of transaction cost theory, which is an extension of the economic analysis which underlies much of the conventional wisdom. It can be argued that a deeper understanding of how and why existing practices have developed is needed.

13.4 Directions for the Future

Progress towards an understanding of the role of management accounting in practice is likely to come from a suitable blend of economic (e.g., agency theory) and organisational and behavioural approaches to research. To exploit these approaches to the full there is a need for collaborative research in which researchers trained in economics, organisation theory, behavioural science, etc., as well as accounting, study the practice of management accounting.

In addition to providing information for decision making, management accounting in practice forms part of a system of organisational control which maintains the direction and cohesion of the organisation – as a result, it has behavioural and political dimensions. For instance, accounting information may be used in bargaining processes, such as bargaining for shares of capital resources available for investment, and for justifying actions already taken. Accordingly, before real progress can be made in closing the gap between theory and practice, researchers must examine the various roles which management accounting fulfils within the organisation.

In view of this need to understand existing practices and to bring theory and practice closer together, some comments are needed about the complexity of information economics research. The mathematical analysis of agency theory, game theory and information economics in general is highly theoretical and at times it is very difficult to discern the implications for the study of management accounting (as distinct from the study of mathematics). Such complexities have given rise to concern. One frequent criticism of much published accounting research in this area is that it is largely unintelligible to practitioners (and also to many students and academics).

Although the initial application of information economics in management accounting, as summarised by Demski and Feltham (1976), was intended to provide a framework for selecting accounting systems in practice, it is not intended that currently researched agency theory models should be used by practitioners. These models provide researchers with a means of studying problems and gaining insights into their solution. The development of such models to a state where useful implications can be generated requires considerable intellectual effort, much of which is of immediate interest only to researchers in the area concerned. In these circumstances mathematical expressions can provide a convenient language for the researchers. However, if the research is ultimately to have practical value, it is essential that the practical implications can be explained, demonstrated and 'sold' to practitioners in a language which they (the practitioners) understand. Similar comments could be made about the jargon and methodologies used by most researchers.

Attempts to make all research intelligible, to all practitioners, at all times, will inevitably restrict the development of the subject. But researchers must be prepared to develop their work (or some researchers be prepared to develop the work of others) to a point where the practical implications become intelligible and, more importantly, acceptable to practitioners. Agency theory research has not yet reached this stage. Much of the published work is still concerned with model development and further such work is likely in the future. In addition, there is likely to be an increasing number of behavioural experiments to test agency models. It is to be hoped that these experiments will soon move from student subjects to the real subjects of interest – managers in actual organisations.

Alongside this theoretical research there is likely to be continuing interest in more practically-based research. Such research will probably investigate the role of activity-based costing, explore the potential of non-quantitative indicators and develop concepts and techniques for strategic management accounting. Such practical research, however, will need a more solid theoretical base than management accounting's conventional wisdom. Unfortunately, although the work of agency theory researchers gives some theoretical insights, it does not provide a sufficiently broad-based theoretical framework. The gap between theory and practice is reflected in a gap between theoretical research and practical research. Practical research needs a theoretical framework capable of practical application. Such a framework is most likely to come from studies of existing practice which attempt to develop explanatory theories of management accounting – theories which both explain existing practice and provide the starting point for practical developments. Such theories still elude management accounting researchers.

References

Ackoff, R. L. (1978) 'The Future of Operational Research is Past and Resurrecting the Future of Operational Research', Paper presented at the national meeting of the Operational Research Society (UK), Philadelphia, The Wharton School.

Amey, L. R. (1969) *The Efficiency of Business Enterprises* (George Allen & Unwin).

Amey, L. R. and D. A. Eggington (1973) *Management Accounting: A Conceptual Approach* (Longman).

Argenti, J. (1976) 'Whatever Happened to Management Techniques?' *Management Today* (April) pp. 178–9.

Baiman, S. (1982) 'Agency Research in Managerial Accounting: A Survey', *Journal of Accounting Literature* (Spring) pp. 154–213.

Baiman, S. (1990) 'Agency Research in Management Accounting: A Second Look', *Accounting Organizations and Society*, vol. 15, no. 4, pp. 341–71.

Baiman. S. and J. S. Demski (1980a) 'Variance Analysis Procedures as Motivation Devices', *Management Science* (August) pp. 840–8.

Baiman S. and J. S. Demski (1980b) 'Economically Optimal Performance Evaluation and Control Systems', *Journal of Accounting Research* (Supplement) pp. 184–220.

Baiman, S. and J. C. Noel (1985) 'Noncontrollable Costs and Responsibility Accounting', *Journal of Accounting Research* (Autumn) pp. 486–501.

Banker, R. (1981) 'Equity Considerations in Traditional Full Cost Allocation Practices: An Axiomatic Perspective', in S. Moriarity (ed.), *Joint Cost Allocations* (Centre for Economic and Management Research, Norman, Oklahoma) pp. 110–30.

Banker, R. D. and S. M. Datar (1989) 'Sensitivity, Precision, and Linear Aggregation of Signals for Performance Evaluation', *Journal of Accounting Research* (Spring) pp. 21–39.

Baxter, W. T. (1938) 'A Note on the Allocation of Oncosts between Departments', *Accountant* (5 November) pp. 633–6.

Berry, A. J., T. Capps, D. Cooper, P. Ferguson, T. Hopper and E. A. Lowe (1987) 'Management Control in an Area of the National Coal Board: Rationales of Accounting Practices in a Public Enterprise', in R. Scapens, D. Cooper and J. Arnold (eds), *Management Accounting: British Case Studies* (Chartered Institute of Management Accountants) pp. 217–64.

Biddle, G. C. and R. Steinberg (1984) 'Allocations of Joint and Common Costs', *Journal of Accounting Literature*, vol. 3 (Spring) pp. 1–46.

Bierman, H., L. E. Fouraker and R. K. Jaedicke (1961) 'A Use of Probability and Statistics in Performance Evaluation', *Accounting Review* (July) pp. 409–17.

Bodnar, G. and E. J. Lusk (1977) 'Motivational Considerations in Cost Allocation Systems: A Conditioning Theory Approach', *Accounting Review* (October) pp. 857–68.

Bromwich, M. and A. Bhimani (1989) *Management Accounting: Evolution not Revolution* (Chartered Institute of Management Accountants).

Chandler, A. D. (1977) *The Visible Hand: The Managerial Revolution in American Business* (Belknap).

Chandler, A. D. and H. Daems (1980) 'Administrative Coordination, Allocation and Monitoring: A Comparative Analysis of the Emergence of Accounting and Organization in the USA and Europe', *Accounting, Organizations and Society* (January) pp. 3–19.

Clark, J. M. (1923) *Studies in the Economics of Overhead Costs* (University of Chicago Press).

Coates, J. B. and S. B. Longden (1989) *Management Accounting: The Challenge of Technological Innovation* – CIMA Study No. 1 (Chartered Institute of Management Accountants).

Coates, J. B., C. P. Rickwood and R. J. Stacey (1987) 'The Use of

Cost Behaviour Analysis – Case Study Evidence', in R. Scapens, D. Cooper and J. Arnold (eds), *Management Accounting: British Case Studies* (Chartered Institute of Management Accountants) pp. 169–216.

Coates J. B., J. E. Smith and R. J. Stacey (1983) 'Results of a Preliminary Survey into the Structure of Divisionalised Companies, Divisionalised Performance Appraisal and the Associated Role of Management Accounting', in D. Cooper, R. Scapens and J. Arnold (eds), *Management Accounting Research and Practice* (Institute of Cost and Management Accountants) pp. 265–82.

Cohen, M. D. and J. G. March (1974) *Leadership and Ambiguity: The American College President* (McGraw-Hill).

Cohen, M. D., J. G. March and J. P. Olsen (1972) 'A Garbage Can Model of Organizational Choice', *Administrative Science Quarterly* (March) pp. 1–25.

Cooper, R. (1987) 'Does Your Company Need a New Cost System?', *Journal of Cost Management* (Spring) pp. 45–9.

Cooper, R. and R. S. Kaplan (1988) 'Measure Costs Right: Make the Right Decisions', *Harvard Business Review* (September–October) pp. 96–103.

Cox, B. (1982) 'Management Accounting – What is it?', *Management Accounting* (March).

Cyert, R. M. and J. G. March (1963) *A Behavioral Theory of the Firm* (Prentice-Hall).

Demski, J. S. (1967) 'An Accounting System Structured on a Linear Programming Model', *Accounting Review* (October) pp. 701–12.

Demski, J. (1973) 'The Nature of Management Accounting Research: A Comment', in N. Dopuch and L. Revsine (eds), *Accounting Research 1960–70: A Critical Evaluation* (Centre for International Education and Research in Accounting) pp. 69–78.

Demski, J. S. (1980) *Information Analysis*, 2nd edn (Addison-Wesley).

Demski, J. S. (1981) 'Cost Allocation Games', in S. Moriarity (ed.), *Joint Cost Allocations* (Center for Economic and Management Research, Norman, Oklahoma) pp. 142–73.

Demski, J. S. and G. A. Feltham (1976) *Cost Determination: a Conceptual Approach* (Iowa State University Press).

Dobbins, R. and S. F. Witt (1983) *Portfolio Theory and Investment Management* (Blackwell).

Dopuch, N. (1981) 'Some Perspectives on Cost Allocations', in S. Moriarity (ed.), *Joint Cost Allocations* (Center for Economic and Management Research, Norman, Oklahoma) pp. 1–7.

Dopuch, N., J. G. Birnberg and J. Demski (1967) 'An Extension of Standard Cost Variance Analysis', *Accounting Review* (July) pp. 526–36.

Dopuch, N., J. G. Birnberg and J. Demski (1982) *Cost Accounting: Accounting Data for Management Decisions*, 3rd edn (Harcourt Brace Jovanovich).

Drury, C. (1989) 'Activity-Based Costing', *Management Accounting (UK)* (September) pp. 60–6.

Dyckman, T. R. (1969) 'The Investigation of Cost Variances', *Journal of Accounting Research* (Autumn) pp. 215–44.

Dyckman, T. R. (1975) 'Some Contributions of Decision Theory to Accounting', *Journal of Contemporary Business* (Autumn) pp. 69–89.

Emmanuel, C. and D. Otley (1985) *Accounting for Management Control* (Van Nostrand Reinhold).

Ferrara, W. L. (1964) 'Responsibility Accounting – A Basic Control Concept', *NAA Bulletin* (September) pp. 11–22.

Finnie, J. and J. Sizer (1983) 'The Apparent Value Placed upon Product Cost Information in a Sample of Engineering Companies', in D. Cooper, R. Scapens and J. Arnold (eds), *Management Accounting Research and Practice* (Institute of Cost and Management Accountants) pp. 307–17.

Fremgen, J. and S. Liao (1981) *The Allocation of Corporate Indirect Costs* (National Association of Accountants).

Green, T. B., W. B. Newsom and G. R. Jones (1977) 'A Survey of the Application of Quantitative Techniques to Production/ Operations Management in Large Corporations', *Academy of Management Journal* (December) pp. 669–76.

Gregory, G. and J. Piper (1983) 'A Study of the Raw Material Reorder Decisions in Small Batch Manufacturing Companies', in D. Cooper, R. Scapens and J. Arnold (eds), *Management Accounting Research and Practice* (Institute of Cost and Management Accountants) pp. 318–62.

Gynther, R. S. (1963) 'Improving Separation of Fixed and Variable Expenses', *NAA Bulletin* (June) pp. 29–38.

Hartley, R. V. (1968) 'Operations Research and Its Implications for the Accounting Profession', *Accounting Review* (April) pp. 321–32.

Hartley, R. V. (1971) 'Decision Making when Joint Products are Involved', *Accounting Review* (October).

Holmstrom, B. (1979) 'Moral Hazard and Observability', *Bell Journal of Economics* (Spring) pp. 74–91.

Holmstrom, B. (1982) 'Moral Hazard in Teams', *Bell Journal of Economics* (Autumn) pp. 324–40.

Hopwood, A. (1979) 'Editorial', *Accounting, Organizations and Society*, vol. 4, no. 3, pp. 145–7.

Horngren, C. T. (1975) 'Management Accounting: Where are We?' in *Management Accounting and Control* (University of Wisconsin-Madison).

Horngren, C. T. (1977) *Cost Accounting: a Managerial Emphasis*, 4th edn (Prentice-Hall).

Horngren, C. T. and G. Foster (1987) *Cost Accounting: A Managerial Emphasis*, 6th edn (Prentice–Hall).

Hunt, R., L. Garrett and C. M. Merz (1985) 'Direct Labor Cost Not Always Relevant at H–P', *Management Accounting (US)* (February) pp. 58–62.

Innes, J. and F. Mitchell (1989) *Management Accounting: The Challenge of Technological Innovation* – CIMA Study No. 2 (Chartered Institute of Management Accountants).

Innes, J. and F. Mitchell (1990) *Activity-Based Costing: A Review with Case Studies* (Chartered Institute of Management Accountants).

Jacobs, F. H. (1978) 'An Evaluation of the Effectiveness of Some Cost Variance Investigation Models', *Journal of Accounting Research* (Spring) pp. 190–203.

Jaedicke, R. K. (1961) 'Improving Break-Even Analysis by Linear Programming', *NAA Bulletin*, Section 1 (March).

Jaedicke, R. K. and A. A. Robichek (1964) 'Cost–Volume–Profit Analysis under Conditions of Uncertainty', *Accounting Review* (October) pp. 917–26.

Jensen, D. L. (1973) 'Hartley's Demand–Price Analysis in a Case of Joint Production', *Accounting Review* (October).

Johnson, G. L. and S. S. Simik (1971) 'Multiproduct C–V–P Analysis under Uncertainty', *Journal of Accounting Research* (Autumn).

Johnson, H. T. (1980) 'Markets, Hierarchies and the History of Management Accounting', paper presented at the Third International Congress of Accounting Historians, London Business School (August).

Johnson, H. T. (1983) 'The Search for Gain in Markets and Firms: A Review of Historical Emergence of Management Accounting Systems', *Accounting, Organizations and Society*, vol. 8, no. 2/3, pp. 139–46.

Johnson, H. T. and R. S. Kaplan (1987) *Relevance Lost – The Rise and Fall of Management Accounting* (Harvard Business School Press).

Johnston, J. (1984) *Econometric Methods*, 3rd edn (McGraw-Hill).

Kaplan, R. S. (1969) 'Optimal Investigation Strategies with Imperfect Information', *Journal of Accounting Research* (Spring) pp. 32–43.

Kaplan, R. S. (1977) 'Application of Quantitative Models in Managerial Accounting: A State of the Art Survey', in *Management Accounting – State of the Art* (Robert Beyer Lecture Series: University of Wisconsin-Madison) pp. 30–71.

Kaplan, R. S. (1981) 'Cross-Fertilization of Accounting Research and Practice, Management Accounting', paper presented at Arthur Young Professors' Roundtable.

Kaplan, R. S. (1982) *Advanced Management Accounting* (Prentice-Hall).

Kaplan, R. S. and A. A. Atkinson (1989) *Advanced Management Accounting* 2nd edn (Prentice–Hall).

Kaplan, R. S. and G. L. Thompson (1971) 'Overhead Allocation Via Mathematical Programming Models', *Accounting Review* (April) pp. 352–64.

Kiani-Aslani, R. (1977–8) 'Do Corporate Controllers Use Quantitative Tools Currently Taught in Managerial Accounting?', *Accounting Journal* (Winter), pp. 278–94.

Klammer, T. (1973) 'The Association of Capital Budgeting Techniques with Firm Performance', *Accounting Review* (April) pp. 351–64.

Littler, D. A. and R. C. Sweeting (1989) *Management Accounting: The Challenge of Technological Innovation* – CIMA Study No. 3 (Chartered Institute of Management Accountants).

McClenon, P. R. (1963) 'Cost Finding Through Multiple Correlation Analysis', *Accounting Review* (July) pp. 540–7.

Maddala, G. S. (1988) *Introduction to Econometrics* (Macmillan).

Magee, R. P. (1975) 'Cost–Volume–Profit Analysis, Uncertainty and Capital Market Equilibrium', *Journal of Accounting Research* (Autumn).

Magee, R. P. (1976) 'A Simulation Analysis of Alternative Cost Variance Investigation Models', *Accounting Review* (July) pp. 529–44.

Marschak, J. and R. Radner (1972) *Economic Theory of Teams* (Yale University Press).

Miller, J. G. and T. E. Vollmann (1985) 'The Hidden Factory', *Harvard Business Review* (September–October) pp. 142–50.

Mood, A., F. Graybill and D. Boes (1974) *An Introduction to the Theory of Statistics*, 3rd edn. (McGraw-Hill).

Moriarity, S. (1975) 'Another Approach to Allocating Joint Costs', *Accounting Review* (October) pp. 791–5.

National Association of Accountants (1960) 'Separating and Using Costs as Fixed and Variable', *NAA Accounting Practice Report No. 10*, reprinted as *NAA Bulletin* (June), Section 3.

National Association of Accountants (1981) 'Definition of Management Accounting', *Statements on Management Accounting*, no. 1A (March 19).

Otley, D. T. (1980) 'The Contingency Theory of Management Accounting: Achievement and Prognosis', *Accounting, Organizations and Society*, vol. 5, no. 4, pp. 413–28.

Otley, D. T. (1984) 'Management Accounting and Organization Theory: A Review of their Interrelationship', in R. W. Scapens, D. T. Otley, and R. J. Lister (eds), *Management Accounting, Organizational Theory and Capital Budgeting* (Macmillan/ ESRC) pp. 96–164.

Perks, R. W. and J. B. Morrell (1981) 'Management Accounting on Degree Courses in UK Universities and Polytechnics', *AUTA Review* (Spring) pp. 31–41.

Primrose, P. L. (1988) 'AMT Investment and Costing Systems', *Management Accounting (UK)* (October) pp. 26–7.

Raun, D. L. (1964) 'The Limitations of Profit Graphs, Break-Even Analysis and Budgets', *Accounting Review* (October) pp. 927–45.

Roberts, J. and R. Scapens (1987) 'Two Case Studies of Accounting and Control in Divisionalised Organisations', in R. Scapens,

D. Cooper and J. Arnold (eds), *Management Accounting: British Case Studies* (Chartered Institute of Management Accountants) pp. 295–314.

Samuels, J. M. (1965) 'Opportunity Costing: An Application of Mathematical Programming', *Journal of Accounting Research* (Autumn) pp. 182–91.

Scapens, R. W., D. Cooper and J. Arnold (1987) *Management Accounting: British Case Studies* (Chartered Institute of Management Accountants).

Scapens, R. W., M. Y. Gameil and D. J. Cooper (1983) 'Accounting Information for Pricing Decisions', in D. Cooper, R. Scapens and J. Arnold (eds), *Management Accounting Research and Practice* (Institute of Cost and Management Accountants) pp. 283–306.

Shillinglaw, G. (1977) *Managerial Cost Accounting,* 4th edn (Irwin).

Shubik, M. (1962) 'Incentives, Decentralized Control, the Assignment of Joint Costs and Internal Pricing', *Management Science* (April) pp. 325–43.

Simon, H. A. (1960) *The New Science of Management Decision* (Harper & Row).

Simon, H. A., H. Guetzkow, G. Kozmetsky and G. Tyndall (1954) *Centralization Versus Decentralization in Organizing the Controller's Department* (Controllership Foundation).

Solomons, D. (1965) *Divisional Performance: Measurement and Control* (Financial Executives Research Foundation)

Spicer, B. H. (1990) 'New Directives in Management Accounting Practice and Research', *Management Accounting Research* (June) pp. 139–46.

Spicer, B. H. and Van Ballew (1983) 'Management Accounting Systems and the Economics of Internal Organization', *Accounting, Organizations and Society*, vol. 8, no. 1, pp. 73–96.

Suh, Y. (1987) 'Collusion and Noncontrollable Cost Allocation', *Journal of Accounting Research* (supplement) pp. 22–46.

Suh, Y. (1988) 'Noncontrollable Costs and Optimal Performance Measurement', *Journal of Accounting Research* (Spring) pp. 154–68.

Sundem, G. L. (1974) 'Evaluating Simplified Capital Budgeting Models Using a Time-state Preference Metric', *Accounting Review* (April) pp. 306–20.

Sundem, G. L. (1981) 'Future Perspectives in Management Accounting Research', paper presented at the Seventh Accounting Research Convocation at the University of Alabama.

Thomas, A. L. (1969) 'The Allocation Problem in Financial Accounting Theory', *Studies in Accounting Research No. 3* (American Accounting Association).

Thomas, A. L. (1980) *A Behavioural Analysis of Joint-Cost Allocation and Transfer Pricing* (Stipes).

Tiessen, P. and J. H. Waterhouse (1983) 'Towards a Descriptive Theory of Management Accounting', *Accounting Organizations and Society*, vol. 8, no. 2/3, pp. 251–67.

Walker, M. (1989) 'Agency Theory: A Falsificationist Perspective', *Accounting, Organizations and Society*, vol. 14, no. 5/6, pp. 433–53.

Weick, K. E. (1969) *The Social Psychology of Organizing*, 1st edn (Addison-Wesley).

Weick, K. E. (1979) *The Social Psychology of Organizing*, 2nd edn (Addison-Wesley).

Williamson, O. E. (1975) *Markets and Hierarchies: Analysis and Antitrust Implications* (Free Press).

Zimmerman, J. L. (1979) 'The Costs and Benefits of Cost Allocations', *Accounting Review* (July) pp. 504–21.

Index